THE
FEINGOLD
COOKBOOK
FOR HYPERACTIVE
CHILDREN

THE
FEINGOLD
COOKBOOK
FOR HYPERACTIVE
CHILDREN

and others with problems associated
with food additives and salicylates

BEN F. FEINGOLD, M.D.
&
HELENE S. FEINGOLD

 Random House   New York

All royalties from this book have been donated by the authors to the
Feingold Foundation for Child Development.

Library of Congress Cataloging in Publication Data

Feingold, Ben F., M.D.
The Feingold cookbook for hyperactive children,
and others with problems associated with food
additives and salicylates.

Includes index.
1. Hyperkinesia—Nutritional aspects.
2. Cookery for hyperactive children. I. Feingold, Helene S.,
joint author. II. Title.
RJ506.H9F46   641.5'63   78–21630
ISBN 0–394–41232–X
ISBN 0–394–73664–8 pbk.

Manufactured in the United States of America

2468B9753

ILLUSTRATIONS BY PAT STEWART

ACKNOWLEDGMENTS

I wish to acknowledge the assistance of the members of the Feingold associations of the United States and parents of children throughout Australia and Canada following the Feingold Path who sent me hundreds of recipes and their local cookbooks. I am most grateful and wish I could have used them all.

I am equally indebted to my colleagues, members of the Brandeis University National Women's Committee who gave me permission to use the excellent recipes in their local chapters' cookbooks. My friends in San Francisco were most gracious, too, in giving me their treasured recipes.

I am particularly appreciative of the assistance of Elaine Schaefer of the Long Island Association, Ruth Sabo of Albany, Gerrie Masters of Baytown, Texas, and my good friend, a gourmet cook, Minette Sissman of Memphis, Tennessee, who shared her prized recipes. I thank them all. I also wish to acknowledge to Mary Ann Malcolm my appreciation for her assistance, and I am indebted, too, to our granddaughter Paula Mayer. The Feingold girls in the allergy department of Kaiser-Permanente Medical Center were helpful in testing many of the recipes for baked goods. I am appreciative of the gracious assistance I have received from so many interested in the welfare of the world's troubled children.

HELENE S. FEINGOLD

THIS BOOK IS DEDICATED TO THE MANY PARENTS WHO,
BY SHARING THEIR SUCCESS WITH OTHER FAMILIES,
MADE VALID THE CONCEPT OF DIETARY MANAGEMENT

CONTENTS

INTRODUCTION 3

SOME HINTS FOR AND FROM PARENTS
FOLLOWING THE FEINGOLD DIET 25

APPETIZERS AND SNACKS 49

SOUPS 71

FOWL 83

MEAT 103

FISH AND SEAFOOD 137

SAUCES AND CONDIMENTS 149

VEGETABLES 163

RICE, NOODLES, AND PASTA 191

SALADS AND SALAD DRESSINGS 209

EGGS AND CHEESE 231

BREADS 239

BEVERAGES 265

CAKES 271

COOKIES 283

PIES AND OTHER DESSERTS 297

INDEX 319

INTRODUCTION

In June 1973 I presented the preliminary observations on the dietary management of hyperkinetic and learning-disabled children before the Allergy Section of the annual meeting of the American Medical Association in New York.

The presentation caught the attention of correspondents and science writers, which led to considerable coverage by the national news media—the press, radio, and TV. Within a few weeks I began to receive inquiries as well as case histories from parents, physicians, psychologists, psychiatrists, teachers, educators, universities, and government agencies. Shortly thereafter I wrote the book, *Why Your Child Is Hyperactive*.

Now, several years later, the interest has not abated. Not only has the number of inquiries increased, they now come from beyond our borders to include Canada, England, Sweden, Norway, France, Germany, Greece, Israel, Saudi Arabia, South Africa, Mexico, New Zealand, Australia, and Japan.

No longer are all the letters plaintive cries expressing desperation ("For God's sake, please help!") or guilt ("What have we done wrong?"). There are now growing numbers of success stories, often dramatic, in response to dietary management. Instead of distraught parents and a disrupted home, the family life is now serene and happy; instead of conflict with peers, the children enjoy the companionship of playmates; instead of failure and frustration at school, the children's scholastic performance is not only satisfactory but frequently reported as excellent. All this is achieved without the crutch of medication, which masks the underlying condition and cures nothing. The experiences of the many thousands of children, their parents, and their teachers have led to a sharpening of our understanding of this complex clinical pattern. We have learned from the many questions and problems that at times confront parents when they undertake dietary management for their children. Those questions are the basis for many of the answers that follow.

How do you know your child is hyperactive? If a child's behavior is extremely disturbed, no professional advice may be required to make a diagnosis. Symptoms of sleeplessness, hyperactivity, aggressiveness, destructiveness, abusiveness, short attention span, and inability to concentrate for more than a few moments are obvious.

Occasionally, the child may not be particularly hyperactive but may have an assortment of other deficits, for example, short attention span, inability to concentrate, aggression, and so on. Such children may fail to do well at school.

Some children do not manifest a marked disturbance in the behavioral pattern but do poorly at school. In such cases we have observed that a trial period with the diet for about one month may be followed by improved performance at school. For such children dietary control should be continued.

Some children may show improved behavior on the diet but remain deficient in a single subject, for example, math or reading. In such cases the behavior may be controlled at home but not at school. It is advisable, through appropriate professional testing, to determine the nature of the child's deficit and to offer one-to-one instruction in addition to the diet.

At times it is difficult to differentiate normal childhood exuberance from hyperactivity. Various psychological tests are not too reliable for a diagnosis in this group of children. If in doubt, there is no harm in trying the diet for a period of a few weeks to a month. There is no risk with the diet. If the diet is tried, strict compliance must be observed—it cannot be a partial trial. A decided improvement in the child's behavior or performance at school serves as an indication that the child may be having minor problems that dietary control can correct.

THE FEINGOLD DIET

Two groups of foods are eliminated by the Feingold Diet.

Group I is made up of all foods that contain synthetic (artificial) colors and synthetic (artificial) flavors, as well as two preservatives—the antioxidants butylated hydroxytoluene (BHT) and butylated hydroxyanisole (BHA).

It is not practical to compile a list of all foods and beverages containing these additives. The safest approach is to read the labels carefully. Most "permitted" food items are available in regular markets. It is usually not necessary to pay premium prices at specialty food stores.

Synthetic (artificial) colors may be listed as U.S. certified, certified, FD&C approved, USDA (U.S. Department of Agriculture) approved. Each of these terms indicates synthetic or artificial color.

Synthetic (artificial) flavors may be listed as "flavoring" or "artificial flavoring." Both types should be eliminated.

Note: Vanillin is usually a synthetic product. Caramel either as a coloring or as a flavoring is usually chemically treated and should be eliminated.

Most vitamin preparations and pediatric medications contain artificial coloring or flavoring or both.

Malt flavoring should be eliminated.

Butylated hydroxytoluene (BHT) and butylated hydroxyanisole (BHA) are antioxidant preservatives used to prevent oils and fats from going rancid. They are very commonly incorporated into cooking fats, cooking oils, foods with an oil or fat content, and packaging materials. When used in packaging, the BHT and BHA leach into the food.

The BHT and BHA used in packaging may not be listed in the ingredients on the package but may be indicated in a separate statement. Be sure to read the labels carefully. *If in doubt, do not use the product.*

BHT and BHA are frequently not disclosed on the package. This occurs very often when BHT and BHA are incorporated into an ingredient used for preparing the food or beverage.

For example, BHT may be introduced into a shortening by the manufacturer of the shortening. When the shortening with BHT is used by the baker for breads, cookies, crackers, and so on, the BHT will not be disclosed, because the baker did not introduce the BHT.

BHT may be incorporated into annatto and beta-carotene, colorings used in dairy products, particularly butter and margarine. The BHT is not disclosed on the package for these products. Caution must be exercised when using dairy products in order to avoid BHT.

Vitamins added to "fortify" or "enrich" a product may be preserved with BHT or BHA and not be disclosed on the package.

Vitamin A, D, or E preparations frequently contain BHT.

Because of this complexity, Feingold associations that have sprung up around the country are fulfilling a very important function by researching the local food supplies and, when necessary, contacting manufacturers for ingredients in their products. Products from the same manufacturer may vary from region to region. In addition, at times manufacturers change their formulae or recipes. For this reason it is not possible to compile a universal list of permissible foods.

The Feingold Association of the United States is divided into regions, each of which compiles a list of permissible foods available in its area. To obtain this information, send a *stamped,* self-addressed envelope to: The Feingold Foundation for Child Development, 1050 North Point Street, San Francisco, California, 94109.

The foods in *Group II* comprise a number of fruits and vegetables that contain natural salicylates (see page 13 for a discussion of salicylates).

The following fruits, vegetables, and miscellaneous items contain salicylates and should be eliminated:

Almonds	Grapes and raisins (also wine and
Apples (also cider and	wine vinegar)
cider vinegar)	Green peppers (also chilies)
Apricots	Nectarines
All berries	Oranges
Cherries	Peaches
Cloves	Plums and prunes
Coffee	Tangerines
Cucumbers and	All teas
pickles	Tomatoes
Currants	Oil of wintergreen

In addition the following sundry items should be eliminated:

Practically all pediatric medications and vitamins contain artificial colors and flavors (see page 18 regarding medications).

Vitamins added to fortify foods may contain BHT or BHA. This is especially true of vitamin A. The BHT and BHA may not be disclosed on the label.

Most over-the-counter medications contain aspirin (acetylsalicylic acid) as well as artificial colors and flavors.

All toothpastes and toothpowders.

All mouthwashes, cough drops, and lozenges.

Perfumes and most aromatic sprays, for example, deodorizers, disinfectants, and insecticides.

All chewing gums contain BHT, and sugarless gum also contains synthetic flavors and, at times, colors.

Finger paints and play dough used by children at home, nursery school or kindergarten contain artificial coloring. This coloring is introduced into the mouth by hands and fingers contaminated with the color.

PROCEDURE FOR FOLLOWING THE FEINGOLD DIET

STAGE I

Eliminating entirely both Group I and Group II from the diet at the very beginning of the program offers the greatest assurance of a successful response.

Keep a precise diet diary of all foods, beverages, and medications, which can be checked in the event of an accidental error. Also note behavioral changes.

A successful response depends upon 100 percent compliance. The slightest infraction may lead to failure; a single bite or a single drink can cause an undesired response that may persist for seventy-two hours or more. An infraction on Sunday and then again on Wednesday can keep a child in a persistent state of disturbed behavior throughout the week.

There are no tests to determine whether a child will show an unfavorable behavioral response to any item in either Group I or Group II. Allergy skin tests are not applicable to this problem.

Occasionally a child will show an intolerance to an item not on the list. When this is suspected, the food should be eliminated.

We see the greatest success when the entire family adheres to the diet. A child cannot be expected to stay strictly on a diet when tempted by forbidden items around the house, in the cupboards, and in the refrigerator. This program should present no special hardship to the other family members, since the elimination of nonessential additives is frequently beneficial both to children and to adults of all ages. In addition, the all-out effort by all family members serves as an added incentive for the child.

STAGE II

If a good response has persisted for about four to six weeks, it is then permissible to try to introduce the salicylate-containing fruits and vegetables in Group II. *It must be noted that artificial colors, artificial flavors, BHT, and BHA must always be eliminated.* They are never tried again, never used again.

How long before a favorable response is observed? The time required may vary with each child. As a rule the younger the child the more rapid the response, but there are variations from this rule.

The diet is usually not effective if the child is receiving behavior-modifying drugs. Your physician should be consulted regarding discontinuing medication.

Infants and children up to two years of age may respond within thirty-six hours.

Children from two to five years of age may respond within three to five days.

With children from six to twelve years of age the response may require ten to fourteen days. Children who have been receiving behavior-modifying medication may require thirty to forty days before a favorable response is observed.

Adolescents and adults may require thirty to forty days for a response to occur. Occasionally they may require several months.

Some children do not respond according to these general rules. Occasionally, a two-year-old may require a week or two for a favorable response. On the other hand, a child eleven or twelve years of age or even an adolescent or young adult may manifest improvement within a few days.

Each individual has his or her own pattern. Don't be disturbed if the child deviates from the average in either direction.

Overt salicylate sensitivity is not observed very frequently in childhood; that is, a child may have salicylate sensitivity and not present a marked disturbance in behavior. Therefore, great caution and restraint must be exercised when reintroducing the items in Group II. If a history of aspirin intolerance is present in the family—in one or both parents —great caution must be exercised when testing the individual salicylate-containing foods.

Start with one food at a time. The child may have a favorite, may especially want a tomato or an apple, for example. Try one food at a time for about a week and watch for a reaction.

Be sure to keep a precise diet diary so that in the event that a change in behavior occurs, it can be correlated with the offending food. Record the quantity of the food given. Do not trust to memory for an accurate record; it cannot be done.

If, after one week of testing, no adverse reaction is observed, proceed to test the remaining foods listed in Group II, but test only one food at a time.

Occasionally we see a child who can tolerate one salicylate food but not another. There is no test or procedure to predict tolerance or intolerance. Each child has his or her own pattern, and each food must be tried separately.

Some children manifest a "cumulative effect" for salicylate-containing foods. Apparently, in some children the salicylates build up over a period of time—weeks or even months, depending upon the individual. In this situation a child who has been doing well on the diet, with no infractions, will suddenly have a disturbed behavior. Why this happens is not known, but when it occurs, discontinue all foods with salicylates. After the behavior returns to normal, it is advisable to continue to eliminate salicylate-containing foods, beverages, and medications.

A commonly raised question is whether children outgrow their intolerances. The answer is no.

The behavioral pattern may change as the child passes through puberty, but deficits may persist, particularly those involved in learning, for example, hearing, memory, visual memory, or involvement of the higher centers, as manifested in the reasoning of arithmetic. The persistence of such deficits can lead to behavioral disturbances.

BREAST FEEDING

It is advisable that nursing mothers observe the Feingold Diet, since food additives are secreted in the breast milk and can cause disturbances in the infant.

OTHER FOODS AND CHEMICALS TO CONSIDER

Do other foods and chemicals cause behavioral disturbances? Yes, since any compound in existence, natural or synthetic, can cause an adverse reaction in any individual who is predisposed. Accordingly, nothing is theoretically exempt.

The Feingold Diet focuses upon the commonest causes of behavioral disturbances. Following the diet precisely should lead to a 60 to 70 percent chance to control the child's behavior.

Foods and chemicals not listed in the diet may cause behavioral disturbances but not as frequently. For the child who fails to respond to a careful, strict trial with the Feingold Diet, it is important to look elsewhere. In most such cases it is advisable to consult an experienced professional for guidance.

The following are some commonly used food chemicals about which questions are frequently asked:

Monosodium glutamate (MSG): A flavor enhancer. (Accent is a common brand name.) MSG is a common cause of neurological disturbances, as is seen in what is known as the Chinese Restaurant Syndrome. It is not recognized as a common cause of behavioral disturbances.

Sodium nitrite and sodium nitrate: Used in the preservation of meats, for example, luncheon meats, bacon, ham, bologna, sausages. These are not recognized as causes of behavioral disturbances. However, they are considered as causes of cancer.

Calcium propionate: A mold inhibitor. It has been suspected as a cause of disturbed behavior in some children. This is a chemical to consider if the Feingold Diet has not been successful. However, since it is not one of the more common causes of behavioral disturbance, its routine elimination is not recommended.

Sodium benzoate: A naturally occurring substance that is frequently used as a preservative in foods and beverages. When foods with benzoates, either natural or added as preservatives, are eaten frequently or in large quantities, the chemicals may cause a disturbance in some children. When this occurs, eliminate foods and beverages with added benzoates (usually specified on the label). Benzoic acid is present in some fruits and berries, particularly cranberries.

Other Foods: Chocolate causes adverse reactions but perhaps less frequently than is the common impression. Many times the reaction attributed to chocolate has actually been caused by synthetic chocolate flavoring. Because of the widespread use of synthetic chocolate, great care must be exercised in selecting products with chocolate. There are actually chocolate products marketed that never saw a chocolate (cocoa) bean. (Read labels carefully.) Skin tests and laboratory tests for a diagnosis of chocolate sensitivity are not reliable.

Milk is a common cause of adverse reactions of various types. Some of these adverse reactions are allergic in nature, but very frequently they result from a nonallergic intolerance to milk. There are millions of people in the world who cannot tolerate milk, particularly milk sugar (lactose). Occasionally milk is a cause of behavioral disturbances.

Pork, wheat, corn, and *eggs* are not uncommon causes of adverse reactions, not necessarily in behavior. These adverse responses are usually true allergic reactions.

SALICYLATES

Group II of the diet eliminates a number of fruits, vegetables, beverages, and all medications with a salicylate radical. The interpretation of the term *salicylate* has created a degree of confusion in the minds of some individuals.

Salicylates are a group of compounds related to salicylic acid in their basic structure. These compounds are also related to aspirin but are not identical with it. Originally, salicylic acid was derived from natural sources, first in 1827 from willow bark (*Salix alba*) and then from oil of gaultheria (oil of wintergreen).

In 1860 salicylic acid was first synthesized from phenol.

Since the basic structure of phenol is the benzene ring, many individuals have undoubtedly been misled into thinking that all compounds with a benzene ring are related to phenol, and also that all compounds with a benzene ring react as salicylates. Neither assumption is correct.

Actually, there are many compounds essential to life that are structured on the benzene ring. For example, the benzene ring occurs in several essential amino acids, the building blocks of proteins, which are daily ingested as food. It also occurs in some important neurotransmitters in the body, for example, epinephrine (adrenaline).

Another common misconception is the labeling as a "salicylate" any food that causes an adverse reaction. There are many foods that cause adverse reactions in individuals who are predisposed, but they are not necessarily salicylate-containing foods.

SUGARS

The question is frequently raised, "Does cane sugar cause hyperactivity?" The answer is, sugar does cause hyperactivity in some individuals. However, one must be aware that not only refined cane sugar, but all the simple sugars, which includes brown sugar, beet sugar, corn syrup, molasses, and even honey may play a role in behavior. In a few individuals even white flour, although it is a starch and not a simple sugar, may be at fault in behavior.

The quantity of any sugar that causes hyperactivity will vary from child to child. Therefore, what causes hyperactivity in one child may cause no disturbance in another child.

There are no tests, including the fasting blood sugar test, to determine how much sugar will cause hyperactivity in a child. This should not be confused with the diabetic for whom blood sugar tests can be helpful.

The term "hypoglycemia" is mentioned very frequently. By definition, hypoglycemia means low blood sugar. But what is low?

The normal fasting blood sugar level covers a wide range, from a low of 35 mg/100 ml of blood to a high of 70 mg/100 ml, with an average of about 50 mg/100 ml of blood. Therefore, except for the unusual case with a fasting blood sugar below 35 mg/100 ml of blood, it is usually not possible to label an individual as hypoglycemic on the basis of fasting blood sugar determinations alone. Accordingly, fasting blood sugar tests do not serve as a reliable guide for a child's tolerance or intolerance for simple sugars in behavior.

Then how is the optimal quantity of sugar or sugar products determined for the hyperactive child? It is determined by trial and error. By keeping a diet diary, recording precisely the quantity of each food item taken and the child's behavior, one can, in most cases, soon determine whether too much sugar is causing hyperactivity.

It must be recognized that on an empty stomach the absorption of simple sugars and even white flour is rapid, leading to a lower tolerance. Taken with a full meal, the tolerance for simple sugars may be greater. Therefore, do not offer a child a between-meal snack with a simple carbohydrate load, for example, cakes, cookies, candies, or ice cream, washed down with a bottle of Seven-Up or lemonade highly sweetened with sugar.

In addition to the immediate problems of behavioral disturbance, one must be mindful of the long-term detrimental effects of sugar, for example, predisposition to obesity, diabetes, dental caries, and perhaps even heart disease with hypertension.

We are unquestionably in a "sweet tooth" culture. Cane sugar consumption over the last one hundred years has increased over twenty-fivefold, from four pounds to over one hundred pounds per person per year. Short-term and long-term ill effects have been indicated.

Resolving the carbohydrate problem is contingent upon correcting our cultural food habits, which involves reeducating the taste buds of people of all ages. The ideal program would be to cut down the consumption of all simple sugars immediately, not only cane sugar but also brown sugar, beet sugar, corn syrup, molasses, and even honey. But realistically such a sudden reduction cannot be expected. Perhaps, for those individuals who are already suffering from dental caries, diabetes, or heart trouble such restrictions can be enforced. These individuals are already aware of their problem. However, for the general population a more workable approach would be a gradual phasing out or reduction in the quantity of simple carbohydrates present in the family diet. Within a matter of a few months the palates of the family members will develop a decreased desire for sweets and lose the craving for sugar, which is essential for the successful management of children.

To individuals who are aware of the "sugar problem" some of the recipes in this book may seem quite liberal in the use of sugar. Actually, the recipes call for lesser quantities than are generally used, yet the amount of sweetness is sufficient to make the food item acceptable to the child or adult with a "sweet tooth." It is recommended that over a period of a few months the quantity of sugar, honey, and so on be decreased appreciably by reducing the amount used in recipes or even substituting items that contain no sugar, for example, fruits, vegetables, and nuts.

VITAMINS

The question of whether or not to take supplementary vitamins is very controversial. Most nutritionists and pediatricians agree that on a well-balanced diet supplementary vitamins are not indicated. However, for the very young infant and preschool child it is advised that they receive vitamins A and D. These are available through natural sources, for example, cod liver oil or other fish oils. Pediatric vitamin drops contain artificial colors and flavors.

Vitamin C: Because Group II eliminates some fruits and vegetables, the question of vitamin C deficiency is frequently raised. As you can see in the list that follows, there are many other sources of vitamin C in allowable fruits and vegetables. If in doubt, a single 50 mg white tablet of ascorbic acid will provide the recommended daily allowance (RDA) of vitamin C for a child.

The following are good sources of vitamin C:

Fresh Fruits

guava	grapefruit
papaya	lemon
cantaloupe	pineapple
mango	banana

Raw Vegetables
cabbage
spinach
mung bean sprouts

Cooked Vegetables

broccoli	kohlrabi	peas
brussels sprouts	cauliflower	okra
collard greens	mustard greens	turnips
sorrel	spinach	green lima beans
kale	cabbage	chard leaves
lamb's-quarters	rutabagas	sweet potato
		potato

MEGAVITAMINS

The term *mega* means "great" or "large". Therefore, *megavitamin therapy* means "the administration of inordinate doses of vitamins, many times the usually recommended daily allowance."

From all clinical experience the matter of megavitamins does not relate to behavioral disorders and learning disabilities. There are undoubtedly individuals who require inordinate doses of vitamins, such as those who have some forms of schizophrenia. These are selected cases, so that as a routine procedure the administration of megavitamins is not indicated.

Our position relative to megavitamins is neither complete rejection nor endorsement. Individuals who may require such therapy may be encountered on occasion. In such situations they should be referred to competent practitioners of the art rather than to those with only a superficial understanding.

MEDICATIONS

Most pediatric medications contain artificial colors and flavors. The availability of additive-free medications for children is quite limited.

When medications are indicated, the physician should be apprised of the child's intolerance. Adult preparations free of colors and flavors can be prescribed, but if adult preparations are used, it is important to regulate the dosage to make it suitable for the child.

It is not recommended that over-the-counter preparations be administered to a child without professional guidance.

ALLERGY

Allergy is an inherited constitutional disorder involving the immune system. Intolerance to food additives and salicylates is not an immunological disturbance. Therefore, it is not allergy. It may clinically simulate allergy, but the two are not identical.

Skin tests for food allergy are not reliable and therefore are not recommended. Skin tests for intolerance to food additives have no value. Actually, there are no tests, either clinical or laboratory, to determine an intolerance either to a food additive or to a salicylate.

Allergy commonly does not cause hyperactivity, though in some individuals it may. Allergy usually produces the opposite clinical pattern, one of lassitude, fatigue, tiredness—actually hypoactivity.

If after a careful trial of the Feingold Diet the response is not favorable, and allergy is suspected, it is advisable that a competent allergist be consulted for diagnosis and management.

OTHER CONDITIONS THAT MAY RESPOND TO THE FEINGOLD DIET

I have listed the individual conditions for emphasis. These do not cover all adverse reactions caused by additives. Each of these conditions represents an additional problem for dietary management.

Seizures: Some children with seizures, particularly if they are associated with behavioral disturbances between the seizures, are good candidates for a favorable response to the Feingold Diet.

Some children have very minor momentary psychomotor episodes. The child may halt his or her activity momentarily, eyes fixed staring into space, with a loss of consciousness, the face at times either pale or flushed, followed by a quick return to normal with no awareness that the event occurred. Occasionally, there may be very temporary twitching or jerking.

In some children nightmares and awakening from sleep with frightening dreams may occur.

Some children with seizures will show a response to the Feingold Diet. For such cases it is advisable to *consult your physician* to obtain anticonvulsant medications without colors and flavors. Start the diet; *continue the medication.* If the child responds, having no seizures and improved behavior, under the guidance of your physician slowly reduce the amount of anticonvulsant medication until it is phased out and the child is receiving only the diet.

Retardation: Some children labeled retarded will show a considerable degree of improvement on the Feingold Diet. This is particularly true if behavior is a troublesome feature, since the behavior can very often be controlled by the diet.

Autism: The question of an accurate diagnosis must always be raised in cases of autism.

Children with a diagnosis of autism may show a complete reversal on the diet. It is likely that the diagnosis was not correct in such cases. The behavioral disturbance of the autistic child will frequently respond to the diet.

Gilles de la Tourette Syndrome: Some cases of La Tourette syndrome will respond to the diet. Not every La Tourette is due to additives; however, when additives are the cause, the response is very favorable.

Down's Syndrome: The behavioral component of Down's

syndrome may show a dramatic response to the Feingold Diet. It is certainly worth a trial. There is nothing to lose and much to gain.

Enuresis: Enuresis (bed-wetting), particularly when part of a general behavioral disturbance, will frequently show an early response to the Feingold Diet.

Serous Otitis: Very frequently serous otitis (recurrent fluid in the ears) accompanies the disturbed behavioral pattern. When behavior improves, the serous otitis also shows a favorable response.

Eye Muscle Involvement (Nystagmus, Strabismus): Nystagmus is an involuntary oscillation of the eyeball, usually lateral but sometimes rotary or vertical, often associated with impaired vision.

Strabismus is crossing of the eyes.

Improvement of these conditions has been observed with the Feingold Diet. Although definitive studies on the dietary management of these conditions are still in progress, there is no risk in trying the Feingold Diet. It is advisable to consult with an ophthalmologist for an evaluation of the condition before and after dietary management.

Ben F. Feingold, M.D.

SOME HINTS FOR AND FROM PARENTS FOLLOWING THE FEINGOLD DIET

The use of the Feingold Diet can have a definite effect on the health of not only the hyperactive child but the entire family, so that it becomes a way of life. These recipes have been compiled to make your life not only easier but more enjoyable. No enjoyment of food is lost when following the Feingold Path. These recipes are suitable to use even when entertaining guests, yet they contain nothing that will affect adversely anyone on the Feingold Diet.

In compiling this cookbook from recipes sent me from all over the United States, Canada, and Australia, the only difficulty I found was in limiting the number for use in the book.

Children or adults on the Feingold Path find plenty of delicious foods that they can safely eat. This book, I hope, will prove that.

The recipes have all been kitchen-tested.

Remember to consult frequently the lists of permitted and forbidden foods on pages 5–8. Read labels very carefully, *always*. If the label does not have the necessary information, ask the store personnel what is in the food, though often the store may not have the information. This may also be true when you buy bread and cakes from a local bakery, prepared sauces, salads and meats from the delicatessen, and so on. In most cases, it may be necessary and safer to make your own, as more and more parents are learning to do. Before starting the diet, consult the Feingold Survival Handbook (pages 26–46) to help you through the first weeks.

While it is helpful to have all the latest gadgets and finest equipment in your kitchen, they are not really essential for preparing a fine, wholesome meal. My electric eggbeater was the first to come on the market some fifty years ago. It is a Dormeyer, it is still in good working condition, and I still use it. The only rolling pin I use is one from our granddaughter's play set. She outgrew it, but I find it useful. I have, at times, used a milk bottle for rolling out dough. I use no cookie or biscuit cutters, just the edges of glasses. One can always improvise.

It is very important to know what we can substitute in a recipe for foods we cannot use or do not have on hand. Consult any good general cookbook, where you will find tables of equivalents for fats, oils, and butter, for different kinds of flours, for cocoa and chocolate, and so on.

Bear in mind that pears can be substituted for apples in all recipes, and they make excellent pies. If a recipe calls for raw apple, use raw firm or green pears.

If a recipe calls for beef or chicken broth, use the recipes on page 71 or use a *pure* canned stock or broth without added color, artificial flavor, flour, BHT or BHA. Some commercial broths contain MSG. If your child is not sensitive to it, it is permissible.

Certain companies make a special effort to emphasize the purity of their products. For example, in the yogurt market, Dannon has additive-free products.

FEINGOLD SURVIVAL HANDBOOK

This four-week diet plan will help you get started. It is designed so that you may get a successful response as soon as possible after the start of the diet.

Since the dietary habits of families vary so greatly, there are probably a number of permissible foods not included in this diet plan. But if you have some favorite foods or recipes, wait until after the trial period before using them. By adhering strictly to the initial trial diet, you will have the greatest opportunity for a successful response.

The blank columns in the charts should be used as a diet diary. This is extremely important as a control. If no changes are made in the diet, draw an arrow across the blank space. Write in any changes or additions, such as snacks, under the column "Additions and Changes." Also, record the child's behavior in the column "Behavior Notes," as well as any other special notes, such as results of a school test or school report or comments like "up until midnight," "conflicts with friends." Please be sure to make these entries immediately, since trusting to memory may risk inaccuracies.

You can obtain practically all the foods listed in the diet at any market in the country. This has been done to minimize shopping time, save energy, and reduce food costs. Except for a few special items, it is usually not necessary to shop at health food stores.

Many of the Feingold associations around the country provide menus for the first few weeks of the child's diet. The following is a modification of the four-week program suggested by the Feingold Association of San Diego, California. These foods are quite typical for the San Diego area, yet they are available anywhere. Although chocolate has been excluded from this four-week starting program, there are many children who tolerate chocolate with no ill effects.

FOUR-WEEK MENU FOR FEINGOLD DIET

MENU	ADDITIONS AND CHANGES	BEHAVIOR NOTES
SUNDAY		
B. Pineapple Juice		
Eggs Scrambled with Cream Cheese		
Toast with Sweet Butter and Honey		
Milk		
L. Burritos (page 115)		
Carrot and Celery Sticks		
Milk		
D. Coleslaw (page 213)		
Baked Fish with Lemon-Butter Sauce (page 139)		
Brown Rice, Fresh Broccoli		
Fig-Carrot Cake, Houston (page 275)		
Milk		
Snacks (page 62)		
MONDAY		
B. Grapefruit		
Butterscotch Oatmeal (page 260)		
Toast		
Milk		
L. Egg Salad Sandwich		

MENU	ADDITIONS AND CHANGES	BEHAVIOR NOTES
Pear		
Allen's Lemonade Cookies (page 289)		
Milk		
D. Tossed Salad (Lettuce, Bean Sprouts, White Distilled Vinegar, and Pure Vegetable Oil)		
Hamburger-Potato Pie (page 115)		
Frozen Peas		
No-Knead Refrigerator Rolls (page 250)		
Pure Ice Cream		
Snacks (page 62)		
TUESDAY		
B. Pear Juice		
Betti's Granola (page 63)		
L. Pure Peanut-Butter–Jelly Sandwich		
Hard-Boiled Egg		
Pure Corn Chips		
Banana		
Milk		
D. Avocado on Lettuce Salad		
Rice		
Frijoles with Grated White Cheddar Cheese		

MENU	ADDITIONS AND CHANGES	BEHAVIOR NOTES
Really Easy Chicken Livers (page 92) Mexican Bread (page 243) Snacks (page 62)		
WEDNESDAY B. Whole-Wheat Pancakes (page 255) with Pure Maple Syrup L. Tuna Fish Sandwich Pear Milk D. Tossed Salad Susie's Roast Beef Supreme (page 103) Gingered Carrots (page 166) Mashed Potatoes (page 173) with Homemade Gravy Snacks (page 62)		
THURSDAY B. Pineapple Juice Puffed Wheat or Rice Cereal Cinnamon Toast Milk L. Roast Beef Sandwich Homemade May-		

MENU	ADDITIONS AND CHANGES	BEHAVIOR NOTES
onnaise (page 223) or Homemade Mustard (page 158)		
White Cheese Slices		
Dates		
Milk		
D. Delicious Cabbage (page 165)		
Salmon Soufflé (page 141)		
Baked Potato		
Mary Alice's Pineapple Pie (page 299)		
Snacks (page 62)		
FRIDAY		
B. Slice of Melon with Scoop of Plain, Additive-free Yogurt or Grapefruit		
Scrambled Eggs		
Toast		
Milk		
L. Mock Hot Dogs (page 118) with Homemade Mustard (page 158)		
Banana		
Can of Pineapple Juice		
Milk		
D. Lamb Kebabs		

MENU	ADDITIONS AND CHANGES	BEHAVIOR NOTES

(page 123)
Brown Rice
Zucchini
No-Knead Refrig-
   erator Rolls
   (page 250)
Allen's Lemonade
   Cookies (page
   289)
Milk
Snacks (page 62)		

SATURDAY
B. Grapefruit
   Baked French
      Toast (page 261)
      with Pure Maple
      Syrup
   Milk
L. Melted White
   Cheese on Toast
   Oatmeal Cookies
      (page 293)
   Milk
D. Best Baked Beans
      (page 163)
   Hamburgers on
      Buns with
      Homemade
      Mustard (page
      158)
   Carrot and Celery
      Sticks
   Pure Ice Cream
   Milk
   Snacks (page 62)		

MENU	ADDITIONS AND CHANGES	BEHAVIOR NOTES
SUNDAY		
B. Pineapple Juice or Homemade Lemonade		
Pure Yogurt Banana Split with Nuts (any except almonds), Dates, and Pineapple		
Toast with Sweet Butter		
Milk		
L. Hot Tuna Sandwiches (page 145) on Homemade Buns		
Carrot and Celery Sticks		
Cottage Cheese		
Milk		
D. Carrot and Cauliflower Slaw (page 214)		
Chicken with Susan's Crusty Coating Mix (page 94)		
Peas		
No-Knead Refrigerator Rolls (page 250)		
Baked Pears with Vanilla Glaze (page 314)		

MENU	ADDITIONS AND CHANGES	BEHAVIOR NOTES
MONDAY		
B. Pear Juice		
Betti's Granola		
(page 63)		
Milk		
L. Cottage Cheese		
with Pineapple		
in Mini-Thermos		
Cold Baked		
Chicken		
Pure Corn Chips		
Milk		
D. Ruth's Spinach		
and Bean Sprout		
Salad (page 210)		
Skillet Macaroni		
and Cheese		
(page 199)		
Quick-Mix Banana		
Cake (page 273)		
Milk		
Snacks (page 62)		
TUESDAY		
B. Grapefruit Juice		
Eggs in a Basket		
(page 232)		
Milk		
L. Cream Cheese and		
Chopped Olives		
in Pita Bread		
Pure Corn Chips		
Banana		
Milk		
D. Tossed Salad		
Baked Fresh Beef		
Brisket (page		

MENU	ADDITIONS AND CHANGES	BEHAVIOR NOTES
104) Fancy Mashed Potatoes (page 174) Green Beans Pure Ice Cream Milk Snacks (page 62)		
WEDNESDAY B. Grapefruit Waffles (page 260) L. Hard-boiled Eggs Bread with Pure Peanut Butter Carrot and Celery Sticks Pear Milk D. Spinach Salad with Lemon-Oil Dressing (page 225) Sweet-Sour Pork (page 120) Chinese Fried Rice (page 193) Bread Milk Snacks (page 62)		
THURSDAY B. Melon Omelet L. Burritos (page 115) Raw Carrots		

MENU	ADDITIONS AND CHANGES	BEHAVIOR NOTES
Banana		
Milk		
D. Tossed Salad		
Zucchini-Cheese Muffins (page 187)		
Veal Paprika with Noodles (page 128)		
Peas		
Oatmeal Cookies (page 293)		
Milk		
Snacks (page 62)		
FRIDAY		
B. Pineapple Juice		
Puffed Wheat or Rice Cereal		
Toast		
Milk		
L. Pita Bread with Filling of Ground Cabbage and Carrots, Lemon Juice, and Homemade Mayonnaise (page 223)		
Small Can Pear Juice		
Tossed Salad		
D. Gerrie's Favorite Casserole (page 117)		
Homemade Biscuits (page 248)		

MENU	ADDITIONS AND CHANGES	BEHAVIOR NOTES
Cy's San Francisco Cookies (page 285) Milk		
SATURDAY B. Grapefruit Juice Eggs Lemon Bread (page 241) Milk L. Mock Hot Dogs (page 118) Banana Milk D. Carrot-Zucchini Slaw (page 214) Stir-fry Stragoni (page 109) Rice Minette (page 193) Pineapple Custard Slices (page 300) Milk		
SUNDAY B. Pineapple Juice Grilled White Cheese Sandwich on French Bread Milk with Pure Carob Powder L. Hot Chicken Salad (page 218) Carrot Sticks		

MENU	ADDITIONS AND CHANGES	BEHAVIOR NOTES

Bread
Banana
Allen's Lemonade
   Cookies (page
   289)
Milk
D. Tossed Salad
   Meat Loaf (page
   112)
   Scalloped Potatoes
   (page 174)
   Angela's Broccoli
   (page 164)
   French Bread
   Milk
   Snacks (page 62)		

MONDAY
B. Homemade
   Lemonade
   Baked French
   Toast with
   Easy-to-Prepare
   Honey Butter
   (page 261)
Milk
L. Cold Meat Loaf
   Sandwich
   Pineapple Juice
   Oatmeal Cookies
   (page 293)
Milk
D. Layered Salad
   (page 209)
   Ethel's Three-in-		

MENU	ADDITIONS AND CHANGES	BEHAVIOR NOTES
One Casserole (page 132) Pure Corn Chips Milk Snacks (page 62)		
TUESDAY B. Grapefruit Juice Scrambled Eggs Toast Milk L. Sliced White Cheddar Cheese on Buttered French Bread Lettuce Carrot and Celery Sticks Pear Juice Seeds, any kind D. Grapefruit- Avocado Salad (page 216) Chicken with Susan's Crusty Coating Mix (page 94) Brown Rice Sweet Potato Pie (page 298) Milk Snacks (page 62)		
WEDNESDAY B. Pineapple Juice Puffed Wheat or Rice Cereal		

MENU	ADDITIONS AND CHANGES	BEHAVIOR NOTES
with Honey or Brown Sugar (1 teaspoon only)		
Milk		
L. Piece of Cold Chicken with Pita Bread		
Carrots		
Pure Potato Chips		
Homemade Lemonade		
Milk		
D. Patti's Liver Casserole (page 131)		
Mashed Potatoes (page 173) with Sweet Butter		
Brussels Sprouts		
Andrea's Quick Pineapple Bread (page 240)		
Milk		
Snacks (page 62)		
THURSDAY		
B. Grapefruit Juice		
Waffles (page 260)		
Milk		
L. Pure Peanut Butter and Cream Cheese on Homemade Bread		
Cy's San Francisco Cookies (page 285)		

MENU	ADDITIONS AND CHANGES	BEHAVIOR NOTES

Milk
D. Leg of Lamb
   Italienne (page
   125)
   Baked Potatoes
   (bake 2 extra)
   Brussels Sprouts
   Pineapple Fluff
   David (page 298)		

FRIDAY
B. Pear Juice
   White Cheese
   Omelet
   Milk
L. Cold Lamb Sand-
   wich on French
   Bread
   Banana
   Susie's Carrot
   Cookies (page
   287)
   Milk
D. Tossed Salad
   Kathy's Basic
   Chicken Stock
   (page 71)
   Puffy Broiled Fish
   (page 137)
   Cottage Fried
   Potatoes (fry
   Thursday's left-
   over potatoes)
   Peas
   Broiled Grapefruit
   (page 314)		

MENU	ADDITIONS AND CHANGES	BEHAVIOR NOTES
SATURDAY		
B. Pineapple Juice		
San Diego Egg Nog		
(page 268)		
Toast		
L. Tuna Fish Salad		
Sandwich with		
Homemade		
Mayonnaise		
(page 223)		
Pure Corn Chips		
Homemade		
Lemonade		
Milk		
D. Betty's Texas Taco		
Salad (page 219)		
Con Queso Rice		
(page 191)		
Vanilla Pudding		
(page 303)		
Milk		
Snacks (page 62)		
SUNDAY		
B. Grapefruit		
Oatmeal with		
Brown Sugar		
and Milk		
Toast		
Milk		
L. Cream Cheese with		
Grated Carrot		
Sandwich		
Pear Juice		
Milk		
D. Beef Stroganoff		
(page 104)		

MENU	ADDITIONS AND CHANGES	BEHAVIOR NOTES
Alan's Spinach Casserole (page 179) Plain Noodles Pure Ice Cream Snacks (page 62)		
MONDAY B. Pear Juice Omelet Toast Milk L. Pure Peanut Butter with Honey on Pita Bread or French Bread Pure Potato Chips Banana Milk D. Vegetable Salad Deluxe (page 212) Tuna-Macaroni Bake (page 144) Honey-Glazed Carrots (page 166) Inoculation Pudding (page 303) Snacks (page 62)		
TUESDAY B. Pineapple Juice Butterscotch Oatmeal (page 260) Milk L. Cream Cheese with Nuts (any except		

MENU	ADDITIONS AND CHANGES	BEHAVIOR NOTES
almonds) and Shredded Carrots on Pita Bread Pear Juice Granola Cookies (page 294) D. Tossed Salad Kathy's Basic Beef Stock (page 71) Toasty Cheese Bake (page 235) Pure Ice Cream Snacks (page 62)		
WEDNESDAY B. Puffed Wheat or Rice Cereal with Wheat Germ Banana Milk L. Pure Peanut Butter with Cottage Cheese and Lettuce Sandwich Carrot and Celery Sticks Pineapple Juice D. Coleslaw (page 213) Round Steak Barley-Mushroom Pilaf (page 194) Green Beans Milk Snacks (page 62)		

MENU	ADDITIONS AND CHANGES	BEHAVIOR NOTES

THURSDAY
 B. Grapefruit
   Norwegian Pancakes
     (page 256)
   Milk
 L. Chicken Salad
    Spread (page
    92) on Pita
    Bread
   Banana
   Allen's Lemonade
    Cookies (page
    289)
 D. Salad with Lettuce
    and Zucchini
    (sliced like
    cucumbers)
   Baked Haddock
    with Potatoes
    (page 140)
   Asparagus with
    White Cheese
    Sauce
   Snacks (page 62)		

FRIDAY
 B. Grapefruit Juice
   Hot Oatmeal with
    Brown Sugar
    and Milk
   Eggs
 L. White Cheese
    Sandwich
   Pineapple Chunks
   Dates
   Milk		

MENU	ADDITIONS AND CHANGES	BEHAVIOR NOTES
D. Spinach and Egg Salad with Plain, Additive-free Yogurt (page 211) Honeyed Chicken (page 85) Baked Potato Homemade Biscuits (page 248) Susie's Carrot Cookies (page 287)		
SATURDAY B. Melon with Plain, Additive-free Yogurt Hard-boiled Eggs Cinnamon Toast Milk L. Mock Hot Dogs (page 118) Carol Cummings' Potato Salad (page 217) Milk D. Avocado and Lettuce Salad Lamb Patties (page 124) Cy's San Francisco Cookies (page 285) Milk Snacks (page 62)		

APPETIZERS
AND SNACKS

AVOCADO DIP

Save the avocado seed and place it in the dip until serving time to prevent discoloration of the dip.

1 ripe avocado, peeled, pitted, and chopped
¼ small onion, peeled and grated

4 tablespoons pure olive oil
3 tablespoons lemon or lime juice
⅛ teaspoon salt

Place all ingredients in a blender container, and blend at medium speed for 30 seconds. Pour the dip into a serving bowl; cover, and refrigerate. Serve with fresh vegetables or pure tortilla chips. Makes approximately 1 cup.

GUACAMOLE DIP

Use this delicious Southwestern dip with fresh vegetables for a refreshing snack or a mouth-watering appetizer.

1 ripe avocado, peeled and pitted
1 teaspoon lemon juice

1 tablespoon homemade mayonnaise (page 223)
salt and pepper to taste

In a medium bowl, mash the avocado well. Add the lemon juice and mayonnaise, and beat until smooth. Season; cover, and refrigerate until ready to serve. Makes approximately 1 cup.

✂————————————————————

BRUSSELS SPROUTS AND PIQUANT DIP

This is a favorite of vegetable lovers.

1 pound smallest size
  brussels sprouts
2 tablespoons homemade
  mustard (page 158)

½ cup homemade mayon-
  naise (page 223)

In a small saucepan, cook the brussels sprouts in boiling salted water for 4 minutes. Drain, cover with waxed paper, and chill in the refrigerator.

Meanwhile, prepare the dip: In a small bowl, mix the mustard and mayonnaise together well. Just before serving, spear each brussels sprout with an uncolored toothpick, and serve with the dip. Serves 6 to 8.

✂————————————————————

CARROT SPREAD

Keep this spread on hand for the ideal after-school treat and serve it on crackers, as a filling for celery sticks, or on slices of zucchini.

½ cup peeled and grated
  carrots
1 hard-boiled egg, grated or
  pressed through a sieve
½ teaspoon lemon juice

½ teaspoon peeled and
  grated onion
2 tablespoons homemade
  mayonnaise (page 223)

In a small bowl, mix all the ingredients together very well. Cover, and refrigerate until ready to serve. Makes about ¾ cup.

❃ ────────────────────────────

OLIVES IN A BLANKET

This dough can be kept in the refrigerator for several days and used as needed. It is good for appetizers and snacks.

2 cups white Cheddar
   cheese, cut up and
   softened
½ cup sweet butter, softened

1 cup all-purpose flour
1 teaspoon cornstarch
1 6-ounce can pitted black
   olives, drained

In a medium bowl, mash the cheese and butter with a fork until well mixed and smooth. Add the flour and cornstarch, and work the mixture until it forms a dough. Shape it into one or two rolls, wrap in waxed paper, and chill.

When ready to bake, preheat oven to 350°. Slice off a small amount of dough, and mold around each olive. Place on a baking sheet, and bake for about 12 minutes, or until lightly browned around the edges. Makes approximately 70.

❃ ────────────────────────────

JAPANESE WHITE RADISH (DAIKON)

This radish, the daikon, is available in Oriental food markets. It may be served in many ways—peeled and sliced, with vinegar, or in the following recipe.

Keep fresh ginger in your freezer, and use it as needed—it will keep indefinitely.

1 large daikon
¼ teaspoon peeled and
   grated fresh ginger

¼ cup soy sauce
   (check the label)

The day before serving, wash and peel the daikon. Cut into bite-sized pieces, and place in a small bowl.

In a separate bowl, combine the grated ginger and soy sauce. Pour this mixture over the daikon, and refrigerate, covered, overnight. Serve chilled. Keeps for several days. Serves 8.

CHINESE SNOW PEAS

For an unusual hors d'oeuvre, snow peas are delicious and attractive.

Rinse the snow peas well under cold water, snap off the ends, and remove any strings. In a large bowl, blanch the snow peas by pouring boiling water over them; let stand for 1 minute. Drain, cool immediately in the refrigerator, and serve on your vegetable platter with any well-seasoned dip.

STUFFED SNOW PEAS

35 very young snow peas
1 3-ounce package cream cheese, softened
¼ teaspoon dry mustard
1 teaspoon homemade mayonnaise (page 223)
¼ teaspoon salt

Rinse the snow peas well under cold water, snap off the ends, and remove any strings.

In a medium bowl, pour enough boiling water over the peas to cover; let stand for 1 minute; drain. While still warm, open one side of each pod with a sharp knife. Let cool.

In a small bowl, blend together the remaining ingredients. Fill each pod with a small amount of the cream cheese mixture. Chill, covered, in the refrigerator for at least 1 hour.

❀────────────────────────────

PHYLLIS'S VEGETABLE ANTIPASTO

Make this a day or two in advance to get the full flavor. This delicious antipasto can be served as an appetizer or salad or as an accompaniment to meat dishes as a substitute for pickles. Add a pasta and a chicken dish for an Italian dinner that is great!

½ head cauliflower, broken into small flowerets

2 carrots, peeled and cut into long, thin strips

2 stalks celery, cut into long, thin strips

¼ pound green beans, cut into long, thin strips

½ medium zucchini, cut into long, thin strips

¾ cup water

¾ cup white distilled vinegar

¼ cup pure vegetable oil

1 teaspoon pure olive oil

3 small shallots, peeled and finely chopped

½ clove garlic, peeled (optional)

salt and pepper to taste

1 6-ounce can pitted black olives, drained

Scrub all the vegetables well under running water. Put all the ingredients except for the olives into a large pot with water. Bring to a boil, and simmer, covered, for 5 to 8 minutes. Add the olives, and refrigerate, covered, a day or two in advance. Drain well before serving. Makes 1½ quarts.

CHEESE ROLL

1 pound white Cheddar cheese, grated
1 3-ounce package cream cheese, softened
dash of garlic juice (optional)
2 cups pecans, finely chopped

The day before serving, in a large bowl, beat together the cheeses and the garlic juice until well blended. Shape into a roll 1½ inches in diameter.

Cover a double thickness of 11-by-8-by-15-inch waxed paper generously and evenly with the chopped nuts. Place the roll in the center of the paper; carefully bring up the sides of the paper to wrap the cheese roll and coat it with the nuts. Refrigerate, letting the roll ripen for at least 24 hours. Serve with crackers or toast. Serves 12.

CREAM CHEESE AND CHUTNEY

If you need a quick appetizer, this is it.

1 8-ounce package cream cheese
4 tablespoons pineapple or mango chutney (check the label)

Place the cream cheese on a serving plate and let stand at room temperature for at least 1 hour. Spoon the chutney over the cheese, and serve with Armenian cracker bread or toast rounds. Serves 8.

⌘————————————————————————

PAULINE'S CHEESE SURPRISES

These simple little snacks are truly surprising. They look like lace cookies.

½ pound white Monterey Jack or Cheddar cheese

———————————————————————————

Preheat oven to 350°. Grease well a baking sheet, or use a Teflon baking sheet. Cut the cheese into ½-inch cubes. Space them about 3 inches apart on the baking sheet. Bake for 7 minutes, or until the edges become light brown. (Watch carefully—the fat will cook out of the cheese, leaving little spaces, to give the effect of lace.) Store in airtight tins. Makes 3½ to 4 dozen.

⌘————————————————————————

QUESADILLAS

¼ pound white Cheddar or Jack cheese, shredded

5 flour tortillas (check the label)

———————————————————————————

Preheat oven to 350°. Layer the cheese over the tortillas. Fold the tortillas over, and hold them with uncolored toothpicks. Place on an ungreased baking sheet, and bake for 6 to 8 minutes, or until the cheese melts. Serve warm. Makes 5.

MARY'S CHEESE WAFERS

Great for snacks, these wafers are as good as cookies but have no sugar. You can keep this dough in the refrigerator for up to a week and bake as needed.

1½ cups grated white Cheddar cheese
¼ pound sweet butter, softened
1 cup all-purpose flour
pinch of salt and cayenne
1 level teaspoon dry mustard

In a medium bowl, blend the cheese and butter together well. With your hands, work in the flour and seasonings. Turn the dough out onto a lightly floured board, roll out, and shape into one long roll 1½ inches in diameter. Wrap in waxed paper, and refrigerate for at least 2 hours.

Preheat oven to 350°. Lightly grease a baking sheet. Slice the dough into ¼-inch-thick rounds, and place on the sheet about 1 inch apart. Bake for 8 to 10 minutes, or until lightly browned. Makes 12 dozen.

JUDITH'S EASY PARTY SPREAD

This is unbelievably easy to make, and good, too. You can double or triple the recipe to make as many appetizers as needed.

1 medium onion, peeled and finely chopped
1 tablespoon grated Parmesan cheese
2 tablespoons homemade mayonnaise (page 223)
3 slices pure white bread or 18 rye rounds

In a small bowl, mix the onion, cheese, and mayonnaise together well. Spread on the white bread or rye rounds. Place on an ungreased baking sheet, and broil, 3 inches from the heat, for 1 to 2 minutes, or until lightly browned. (Watch carefully to see that they don't burn.) Cool, then cut the bread into sixths. Makes 18 1½-inch squares or rounds.

❁ ──────────

QUICHE LORRAINE

This popular dish can be served as an hors d'oeuvre, for luncheon with a salad, or for Sunday night supper. If using for hors d'oeuvres for many people, use a 9-by-13-inch glass baking pan.

½ recipe Elaine's Piecrust
    (page 297)
½ pound sliced bacon
    (check the label)
½ pound white Swiss
    cheese, grated
4 eggs
½ teaspoon salt

1 tablespoon all-purpose
    flour
pinch of cayenne
nutmeg
2 cups milk
1 tablespoon sweet butter,
    melted

Preheat oven to 375°. Line a 9-inch pie pan with the pastry. In a large skillet, fry the bacon until crisp. Drain on paper towels, and break into small pieces. Sprinkle the cheese evenly over the pastry, and top with the bacon pieces.

In a large bowl, beat the eggs with the salt, flour, cayenne, and nutmeg. Add the milk and melted butter, and mix together thoroughly. Pour over the bacon and cheese. Bake for 40 minutes, or until set. Cut into wedges or small squares. Serve warm. Makes 6 to 8 servings, if wedges, or 24 small squares.

✂ ANCHOVY STRAWS

This recipe hails from Sydney, Australia.

½ cup all-purpose flour   dash of cayenne
¼ cup sweet butter, softened   1 egg yolk
1 ounce anchovy paste   ½ teaspoon lemon juice

Preheat oven to 350°. In a medium bowl, mix together the flour, butter, and anchovy paste. Season with cayenne. Add the egg yolk and lemon juice, and mix together well.

On a well-floured surface, with a floured rolling pin, roll out the pastry ⅛ inch thick. With a sharp, floured knife, cut into strips 3 inches long by ½ inch wide. Place on ungreased baking sheets, and bake for 10 minutes, watching carefully to see that the strips don't burn. Makes about 3½ dozen.

✂ SMOKED SALMON SPREAD

Some stores or delicatessens sell smaller pieces of salmon in packets (check the labels), which are less expensive than slices. These are ideal for this recipe.

¼ pound smoked salmon,   2 tablespoons sour cream
   cut into small bits   1 teaspoon peeled and grated
1 8-ounce package cream   onion
   cheese, softened

In a medium bowl, beat all the ingredients together well. Refrigerate, covered, until needed. (This spread will keep in the refrigerator for several days.) Serve on toasted bagels or stuffed into celery sticks. Serves 8.

⌘————————————————————

HERRING IN SOUR CREAM

This is an easy way to make this popular appetizer, which is much less expensive than the ready-to-serve product.

1 32-ounce jar herring filets *3 medium onions, peeled*
1 pint sour cream, or sour   *and sliced into rings*
  half-and-half if available

Wash each piece of herring well under cold running water. Drain in a colander or sieve.

Place the herring in a large bowl, and add the sour cream and sliced onions. Mix together gently but well. Refrigerate, covered, in a glass jar for at least 3 days. Stir, mixing well, before serving. (Keeps well in the refrigerator for several weeks.) Serve as an appetizer or with boiled potatoes for luncheon. Makes 50 pieces of herring.

⌘————————————————————

CHIPPED BEEF DIP

For a tasty change, try this hot dip, which can be reheated.

*1 8-ounce package cream
  cheese, softened*
½ cup sour cream
*1 3-ounce package chipped
  beef (check the label),
  chopped into small pieces*

*2 tablespoons peeled and
  minced onion*
¼ cup chopped pecans

Preheat oven to 350°. Grease a small baking dish. In a medium bowl, beat the cream cheese and sour cream together until smooth. Add the chipped beef, onion, and pecans, and mix together well. Pour the mixture into the baking dish, and bake for 20 to 25 minutes. Serve warm, with toast or permitted crackers. Serves 8.

COCKTAIL MEAT BALLS

Since these meat balls are baked rather than fried, they save a lot of time and work.

2 pounds ground beef
1 onion, peeled and minced
1 teaspoon salt
2 eggs

1 cup water
1 cup matzo meal
1 teaspoon garlic powder

Preheat oven to 375°. In a large bowl, mix together all the ingredients. Shape into small balls the size of walnuts, and place on an ungreased baking sheet.

Bake for 15 minutes. Remove from oven, and, with a slotted spoon, place the meat balls on paper towels to drain off excess fat, before serving.

To serve, spear uncolored toothpicks through each meat ball, and arrange on a serving tray. Makes about 75.

⌘————————————————————

SAUSAGE BALLS GERRIE

Here is another way to use the Homemade Biscuit Mix on page 248. These balls can be frozen and are great for brunches or parties. If pure sausage meat is not available, ground pork can be mixed at home with desired spices.

*1 pound pure pork sausage
   meat (check the label)
1 pound white Cheddar
   cheese, grated*

*2½ cups Homemade Biscuit
   Mix (page 248)
¾ cup milk
salt and pepper to taste*

———————————————————

Preheat oven to 350°. Grease a baking sheet. In a large bowl, mix together all the ingredients with a fork or spoon. Roll or pat into small balls the size of walnuts, and place these on the baking sheet. Bake for 22 minutes—sausage must be well cooked. Makes 40 to 45 balls.

⌘————————————————————

HOMEMADE DEVILED HAM

For sandwiches or in yogurt.

*½ cup finely chopped or
   ground cooked ham
   (check the label)
¼ teaspoon dry mustard*

*2 tablespoons homemade
   mayonnaise (page 223)
pepper to taste*

———————————————————

In a small bowl, mix together all the ingredients. Refrigerate, covered, until ready to use. Makes ½ cup.

⌘────────────────────────────────

SNACK SUGGESTIONS

Fresh fruits: banana, pear, melon, grapefruit, avocado, papaya, persimmon, guava, fig

Fresh vegetables: carrot sticks, celery, celery sticks with pure peanut butter or cream cheese, zucchini sticks, raw cabbage or cauliflower, broccoli flowerets, Jerusalem artichoke slices

Juices: pear, pineapple, grapefruit

Pure corn chips, pure potato chips, pure carob chips, pure banana chips (check the labels)

Unseasoned Ry Krisp

Sesame honey candy, available in health food stores

Sunflower seeds

Peanuts or any other nuts except almonds

Matzo crackers

Cracker bread, available at some specialty stores and Armenian food shops

Quesadillas (page 55)

Pita bread

Popcorn—plain, sweet-buttered, salted, or candied

Natural cheeses, such as Swiss or Jack, white only

Plain, additive-free yogurt (may be frozen)

Dates

Pure pretzel sticks (check the label)

Rice cakes

Icies from Sybil (page 265)

Puddings (pages 302–307)

Frozen Yogurt or Popsicles (page 310)

Goldfish thins (Pepperidge Farm)

Small-size bagels

Mary Lou, of Warren, Ohio, has a unique snack tray that she offers children in her nursery school. On holidays she has goodies with colors related to the holiday. For example, on Saint Patrick's Day she serves a beautifully arranged platter of honeydew melon, raw green broccoli flowerets, zucchini strips, cabbage, green olives, lettuce, celery sticks, green onions, and tiny brussels sprouts cooked just a few minutes. The children love it. For Christmas she adds red radishes and tiny beets to the greens. For Thanksgiving and Halloween she serves nuts, yellow squash, Japanese persimmon slices, and melon balls. Use your imagination and create trays of color to celebrate any event.

PLAY DOUGH FOR CHILDREN

If you wish to color this dough with a few drops of beet, spinach, or carrot juice, use a little less water.

1 cup all-purpose flour	2 teaspoons cream of tartar
2 tablespoons pure vegetable oil	½ cup salt
	1 cup water

In a large saucepan over medium heat, combine all the ingredients and stir to mix well. Cook, stirring, until the mixture sticks together and forms a large ball. Pour the mixture out onto waxed paper; let cool. Store in a covered container until children are ready to play with it. Makes 2 cups.

BETTI'S GRANOLA

A do-it-yourself recipe that both children and grown-ups like, this can be served as a cereal with milk or as a snack.

3 cups uncooked rolled oats
1 cup sunflower seeds
1 cup sesame seeds
1 cup wheat germ
1 cup honey
½ cup pure vegetable oil
¼ cup soy flour

1 tablespoon pure vanilla
½ cup water
¼ cup chopped dates
(optional)
¼ cup shredded coconut
(optional)

Preheat oven to 350°. Lightly grease a baking sheet. In a large bowl, combine all the ingredients, except the dates and coconut, with the water; mix together thoroughly. Spread the mixture evenly on the baking sheet, and bake for 20 minutes, or until browned. Stir in the dates and coconut if desired. Store in a covered container. Makes about 7 cups.

❦————

SABO SEEDS

For a wonderful midwinter Sunday treat try these delicious maple-syrup-covered nuts.

1½ tablespoons pure
  safflower oil
¼ cup peanuts
¼ cup pumpkin seeds
¼ cup sunflower seeds
¼ cup sesame seeds

¼ cup chia seeds
¼ cup any nutmeats (except
  almonds)
¼ cup shredded coconut
2 tablespoons pure maple
  syrup, or to taste

Heat a large, heavy skillet, add the oil, and swirl to barely coat the bottom of the pan.

Add the peanuts and seeds; roast, stirring often, for about 8 minutes, or until lightly browned. Add the nutmeats and coconut and continue cooking, stirring, until the coconut turns golden, about 3 minutes.

Remove from heat; add the maple syrup, and stir to coat the seeds and nuts lightly. Serve warm. Makes about 1¾ cups.

✠────────────────

SNACK SPREAD

½ cup wheat germ　　　　　¼ cup honey
½ cup pure peanut butter

───────────────────────

In a medium bowl, mix all the ingredients together thoroughly. Spread on bread slices, and serve.

Makes about 1¼ cups.

✠────────────────

YOGURT WITH NONSWEETS

For a delicious and nutritious change of taste, try mixing any of the following ingredients with 1 cup of plain, additive-free yogurt.

½ teaspoon each of homemade mustard (page 158) and
　　sugar
or
1 tablespoon each canned minced clams and chopped chives
or
1 tablespoon homemade deviled ham (page 61)
or
1 tablespoon mashed canned tuna fish
or

2 *tablespoons cottage cheese*

or

1 *teaspoon each grated Parmesan and Romano cheese*

❀————————————————————————

PEANUT BUTTER–YOGURT DIP

Look for the brand of yogurt in your area that is additive-free, and be sure that it is unflavored.

5 *tablespoons pure peanut butter*	3–5 *tablespoons lemon juice, to taste*
1 *cup plain, additive-free yogurt*	¼ *teaspoon salt*

In a medium bowl, combine all the ingredients. With a fork, beat the mixture until smooth and creamy. Refrigerate, covered, until ready to serve. Serve with breadsticks, zucchini sticks, carrot strips, or pure chips. Makes about 1 cup.

❀————————————————————————

GAIL'S PEANUT BUTTER

Commercial peanut butter so often contains BHT, as do salted peanuts. There are a few additive-free brands on the market but it's easy to make your own.

1½ *cups roasted peanuts,*   *salt to taste*
   shelled

Put peanuts into blender, cover and blend to a creamy consistency. Use rubber spatula to keep ingredients flowing into processing blades. Add salt. If mixture seems too dry, add a few drops of pure peanut oil. Makes ¾ cup.

❧————————————————————

PEANUT BUTTER BALLS

Children like Michael in Minneapolis use these like play dough. They sculpt figures and objects, which are then frozen and packed in their school lunch boxes for a treat or for show-and-tell. If you make this recipe for sculpting, omit the vanilla in order to make a more workable dough.

½ cup pure peanut butter
⅓ cup nonfat dry milk
   powder
¼ cup honey
1–2 tablespoons nutritional
   (Brewer's) yeast (optional)

1 teaspoon pure vanilla
¼ cup unsweetened
   shredded coconut, sesame
   seeds, or chopped nuts,
   any except almonds
   (optional)

In a medium bowl, mix all the ingredients together thoroughly. Shape into small balls. Roll in shredded coconut, sesame seeds, chopped nuts, or serve plain.

SOUPS

KATHY'S BASIC BEEF STOCK

Ask your butcher or supermarket to sell you marrow bones —just as your grandmother did—and reserve the cooked soup meat for a dinner meal or for sandwiches.

4 pounds beef shanks, with meat on the bones
2 3-inch marrow bones
3 quarts water
2 medium carrots, cut into thirds
2 medium onions, quartered
2 stalks celery with leaves, cut up
1 bay leaf
2 sprigs parsley
2 teaspoons salt

In a 6-quart kettle, combine the meat and marrow bones with the water. Add the remaining ingredients, and bring to a boil over moderately high heat. Reduce heat, and simmer, covered, for 4 hours. Strain stock; cool, and chill. Store, covered, in the refrigerator, and skim off all fat before using. (If stock gelatinizes in the refrigerator, warm slightly before measuring for the amount needed for use in a recipe.) Makes 2½ quarts.

KATHY'S BASIC CHICKEN STOCK

The cooked chicken meat is great for salads or sandwiches.

1 5-pound stewing chicken, cut into quarters
1 stalk celery with leaves, cut up
3 medium carrots, cut into thirds
1 medium onion, quartered
1 bay leaf
1 sprig parsley
2 teaspoons salt
2 quarts water

In a 5-quart kettle, combine all the ingredients with the water. Bring to a boil over moderately high heat, reduce heat, and simmer, covered, for 3 hours. Strain stock; cool, and chill. Store, covered, in the refrigerator, and skim off all fat before using. (If stock gelatinizes in the refrigerator, warm slightly before measuring for the amount needed for use in a recipe.) Makes 2 quarts.

⌘────────────────────────────

VERY SPECIAL FARINA BALLS

Serve these delicious balls in hot soup. Uncooked farina balls can be frozen and fried just before serving. Whenever a coating of eggs and crumbs is used, add a tablespoon of olive oil to the egg; the crumbs will then adhere better.

¼ cup quick-cooking farina	½ teaspoon paprika
1 cup milk	1 whole egg, beaten
2 egg yolks, beaten	1 tablespoon pure olive oil
½ teaspoon salt	cracker crumbs (check the
½ teaspoon onion juice	label) or matzo meal
1 teaspoon chopped parsley	pure vegetable oil for frying

In a large saucepan, cook the farina and milk together until all the milk is absorbed. (As the farina cooks, it will tend to leave the sides of the pan, forming a ball.) Add the beaten egg yolks, then all the seasonings. Turn the mixture out onto a platter to cool. When cool, shape into very small balls. Mix the whole beaten egg with the olive oil. Roll the formed balls first in the beaten egg mixture, then in the crumbs or meal. In a skillet, heat ½ inch of vegetable oil; add the balls, and fry them. Drain on paper towels. Serves 8.

EGG STRIP SOUP

1 egg
2 tablespoons grated
   Parmesan cheese
2 tablespoons chopped
   parsley
2 tablespoons milk

salt and pepper to taste
2 teaspoons sweet butter
2 cups Kathy's Basic Chicken
   Stock (page 71) or
   canned broth (check the
   label)

In a small bowl, mix together the first four ingredients; season to taste. In a small skillet, melt the butter; add the egg mixture. Cover, and cook over low heat until the egg is firm. Remove carefully, and drain on paper towels. When cooled, cut the egg mixture into strips about 2 inches long. Place the egg strips in a soup pot or individual soup bowls; cover with hot chicken broth. Top soup with more grated cheese, and serve. Serves 2.

✂

MATZO BALLS

Serve in hot chicken soup or as a side dish to meat and poultry.

2 tablespoons melted chicken
   fat
2 eggs, slightly beaten
½ cup matzo meal

1 teaspoon salt
2 tablespoons water
2½ quarts salted water

In a bowl, mix together the chicken fat and beaten eggs. In a separate bowl, mix together the matzo meal and salt; blend this into the egg mixture. When well blended, add

2 tablespoons of water, stirring in well. Cover, and place in the refrigerator for 30 minutes.

In a 3-quart pot, bring salted water to a brisk boil. Reduce heat so that the water is slightly bubbling. Shape the matzo meal mixture into 8 balls, and drop these into the bubbling water. Cover, and cook for 30 to 40 minutes. Makes 8 balls. Serving size: 1 or 2 balls.

HENNIE'S ALSATIAN MATZO BALLS

These are different from the usual matzo balls because they use the whole matzo rather than matzo meal. They are ordinarily served in soup but can also be used as dumplings with meat such as brisket of beef.

For Passover you can add ½ cup finely chopped celery and use the mixture as dressing to stuff a chicken to be roasted.

3 tablespoons rendered chicken fat
3 tablespoons peeled and finely chopped onion
3 regular-size square matzos, soaked in cold water for a few minutes to soften
2 eggs, slightly beaten
⅓ cup matzo meal
⅛ teaspoon ground ginger
⅛ teaspoon pepper
¼ teaspoon salt
Kathy's Basic Chicken Stock (page 71) or canned broth (check the label)

In a heavy skillet, melt the chicken fat, and lightly brown the chopped onion. Squeeze the matzos well to dry. Add them to the skillet, and brown well. Remove from heat, and mix in the eggs, matzo meal, and seasonings. Let cool.

Shape into balls the size of walnuts. (To keep the mixture from sticking, keep your hands wet with cold water.) Place the balls on a plate or platter, cover and refrigerate for several hours or overnight to firm.

To cook, drop the balls into the boiling chicken soup, and simmer, covered, for about 15 minutes. (Always try one ball first to be sure it holds together. If it falls apart, add more meal to the mixture and remake the balls.) Makes about 26 matzo balls.

SPINACH CUSTARD TO SERVE WITH SOUP

1 pound spinach	*2 eggs, beaten*
2 cups milk	*1 teaspoon salt*

Preheat oven to 350°. Grease a shallow baking dish. Rinse and drain the spinach well. Cook it in boiling water until tender, drain, and set aside to cool.

Pour the milk into the baking dish. Add the beaten eggs and salt and mix in the spinach. Bake for 45 minutes. When ready to serve, cut the custard into cubes with a sharp knife, and serve in any clear soup.

CREAMY VEGETABLE SOUP

1 large potato, peeled and diced	*1 teaspoon salt*
	2 cups water
1 medium carrot, peeled and diced	*1 tablespoon sweet butter*
	pepper to taste
1 medium onion, peeled and diced	*⅛ teaspoon garlic salt*
	1½ cups milk
1 stalk celery, diced	

Place all the ingredients except the milk in a large soup pot. Cook over medium heat for 20 minutes.

With a potato masher or rotary beater, mash the vegetables until smooth. Add the milk, and bring to a boil. Serve immediately. Serves 4 to 6.

⌘——————————————

PUREE OF VEGETABLE SOUP

2 *medium onions*
2 *large carrots*
1 *medium turnip*
2 *small parsnips*
3 *large stalks celery*
1 *potato*
¼ *cup sweet butter*
1 *tablespoon all-purpose flour*

1 *quart boiling water*
1 *teaspoon salt*
1 *tablespoon chopped parsley*
¼ *teaspoon cayenne*
crust of one toasted slice of bread

Wash all the vegetables well, peel, and cut them into small dice. In a soup pot, heat the butter; add the onions, and sauté until golden. Add the flour, and mix thoroughly. Gradually pour the water into the pot, stirring constantly. Add all the ingredients except for the potatoes. (If there is not enough water to cover, add a little more.) Simmer, covered, for 2 hours. Add the potatoes, and boil for 15 minutes longer.

Fill a blender container half full with the soup, and purée. Repeat with the remaining soup. Store, covered, in the refrigerator. Reheat in a double boiler before serving. Makes 1½ quarts.

CREAM OF CAULIFLOWER SOUP

1 medium head cauliflower
3 tablespoons sweet butter
1 large onion, peeled and
    finely chopped
½ cup uncooked rice
3 stalks celery, diced
salt and pepper to taste

2 teaspoons chopped chives
2 teaspoons chopped parsley
2 cups Kathy's Basic Chicken
    Stock (page 71) or canned
    broth (check the label)
½ cup heavy cream
Croutons by Cleo (page 246)

Place the cauliflower in a medium pot, and cover with water. Bring to a boil, and cook over medium heat until the cauliflower is tender. Remove the cauliflower, and set aside, reserving the liquid.

In a large pot, melt the butter, and sauté the onion. Add the reserved liquid, rice, and celery. Season with salt and pepper. Simmer about 20 minutes until the rice is tender. Place the mixture, about 2 cups at a time, in a blender container, and blend until smooth. Put the blended mixture back into the cooking pot and add the chives, parsley, and chicken stock. Chop the cauliflower fine, and add to the soup. Stir in the heavy cream. Heat the soup thoroughly but do not boil. Serve hot, garnished with croutons. Serves 6.

JAPANESE CORN SOUP

This is a delicious, simple, quick soup. Save the corn for corn fritters.

1 17-ounce can cream-style
    corn
1 cup Kathy's Basic Chicken
    Stock (page 71) or chicken
    broth (check the label)

1 teaspoon all-purpose flour

Over a large bowl, press the corn through a sieve, pouring ⅓ cup of the chicken stock over the corn to get as much of the corn liquid as possible. Combine the remaining ⅔ cup chicken stock with the corn liquid.

Place the flour in a small saucepan over moderate heat. Slowly stir in the broth mixture. Cook, stirring, until the soup has slightly thickened and is thoroughly heated through. Serves 2.

MASHED POTATO SOUP

1 tablespoon sweet butter
1 small onion, peeled and finely chopped
½ cup White Sauce Mix Minnetonka (page 149)

1 cup milk
1 cup fresh or leftover mashed potatoes
salt and pepper to taste

In a small saucepan, melt the butter. Sauté the onions until transparent.

In a separate bowl, blend the white sauce mix with the milk; beat in the mashed potatoes. Add this mixture to the onions, and heat well, stirring constantly. Season to taste. Makes about 2 cups.

POTATO SOUP

6 large potatoes, peeled and
   cubed
2 carrots, peeled and diced
1 stalk celery, chopped; or
   3 sprigs parsley
1 onion, peeled and chopped

5 cups water
salt to taste
3 tablespoons pure vegetable
   oil or bacon grease
2 tablespoons cornmeal
pepper to taste

In a soup pot, combine the first four ingredients with the water; bring to a boil. Reduce heat, add salt to taste, and simmer.

Meanwhile, in a small skillet, heat the vegetable oil or bacon grease. Add the cornmeal and pepper, and fry until golden brown. Add this to the soup. Add more water if needed. Cover, and cook for 30 minutes, until the potatoes are done. Serves 4.

HEARTY FISH CHOWDER

2–3 potatoes, peeled and
   cubed
1 cup water
1–2 onions, peeled and diced
1 cup fresh mushrooms,
   sliced
3 tablespoons pure vegetable
   oil or sweet butter
½ cup whole-wheat flour

1 quart skim or whole milk
1 pound filet of fish, cut into
   cubes
1 teaspoon salt
¼ teaspoon pepper
2 tablespoons soy sauce
   (check the label)
3 tablespoons chopped
   parsley

In a covered saucepan, cook the potatoes in the water until tender. Set aside—do not drain. In a large pot, lightly sauté the onions and mushrooms in oil or butter. Add the flour slowly, stirring constantly. Add the milk slowly, again stirring constantly, until the mixture is smooth. Add the fish, salt, pepper, and soy sauce. Cover the pan, and simmer for about 15 minutes, or until the fish is tender, stirring occasionally. Add the potatoes along with their cooking water and the parsley. Heat through. Serves 6 to 8.

FOWL

ROAST CHICKEN

This recipe is for a large fryer, since roasting chickens are difficult to find in today's markets.

1 4-pound chicken
salt and pepper to taste
Italian Stuffing Lynn (page 99)

4 tablespoons sweet butter or chicken fat

Preheat oven to 350°. Season the chicken well, inside and out, with salt and pepper. Stuff with the dressing, and rub 2 tablespoons of the butter or chicken fat over the entire skin surface.

Place the chicken, *breast down,* on a rack in an open baking pan. Add ½ cup of hot water to the pan. Roast until the back is well browned and crisp—about 25 minutes. Turn breast side up, brush with the remaining 2 tablespoons butter or fat, and roast for another 35 to 45 minutes. The breast should be tender when touched with a fork (older chickens may take longer). Serves 4.

CHICKEN WITH PEARS

½ cup pure vegetable oil
1 10-ounce package frozen tiny onions, thawed and drained
2 3-pound chickens, quartered

thyme, salt, and pepper to taste
1 29-ounce can pears
¼ cup lemon juice
chopped parsley for garnish

Preheat oven to 350°. In a large skillet, heat the oil, and sauté the onions lightly; remove onions to a roasting pan. In the same skillet, brown the chicken. Season with thyme, salt, and pepper, and place in the roasting pan.

Drain the pears, reserving the juice; set aside. Mix the lemon juice with the pear syrup, adding more lemon juice if necessary (syrup should be tangy).

Bake the chicken for 1 hour, basting frequently with the pear syrup to give the chicken a nice glaze. Arrange the chicken, onions, and pears on a platter; sprinkle with chopped parsley. Serves 6 to 8.

✂—————————————————————

JAPANESE CHICKEN BAKED IN FOIL

1 3-pound chicken, quartered
2 tablespoons white sesame seeds
3 green onions, including the tops, finely chopped
1 teaspoon sugar
½ cup soy sauce (check the label)
1 tablespoon pure vegetable oil
¼ teaspoon pepper
½ lemon, thinly sliced
Hot Rice (page 191)

———————————————————————

Wash the chicken thoroughly, and pat dry with paper towels. In a dry skillet, toast the sesame seeds just until they begin to jump; watch carefully that they don't burn. Remove from pan. Crush the seeds in a mortar with a pestle, in a blender, or in a nut grinder.

In a shallow glass baking dish, mix together the ground sesame seeds, green onions, sugar, and soy sauce. Marinate the chicken pieces in this mixture for 30 minutes, turning the chicken once.

Meanwhile, cut pieces of foil large enough to wrap each piece of chicken securely. Rub the foil with the oil.

Preheat the oven to 350°. Place a piece of chicken in the center of each piece of foil; sprinkle each with a pinch of the pepper, and top with a slice of lemon. Wrap tightly. Bake for 30 to 40 minutes, or until the chicken is tender. Serve with Hot Rice. Serves 4.

⌘————————————————

HONEYED CHICKEN

2 eggs
2 tablespoons water
1 cup matzo meal
1 teaspoon salt
pepper to taste
2 small chicken fryers,
    cut up

½ cup pure peanut oil
1 cup hot water
¼ cup honey
1 cup unsweetened
    pineapple juice

Preheat oven to 325°. In a small bowl, beat the eggs with 2 tablespoons of water, and set aside. In a separate bowl, mix the matzo meal, salt, and pepper. Dip each piece of chicken into the egg mixture, then roll in the matzo meal mixture.

In a large skillet, slowly heat the oil. Brown the chicken on both sides, and remove to a covered roaster. In a small bowl, combine the hot water, the honey, and the pineapple juice; mix together well. Pour this mixture over the chicken.

Bake for about 45 minutes, or until tender, basting with the juices occasionally. Serves 6 to 8.

OVEN-FRIED CHICKEN WITH LEMON SAUCE

½ cup lemon juice
¼ cup pure vegetable oil
2 tablespoons grated lemon
    rind
1 tablespoon soy sauce
    (check the label)
½ teaspoon salt

½ teaspoon pepper
½ cup all-purpose flour
1 teaspoon salt
2 teaspoons paprika
1 3-pound chicken, cut up
½ cup sweet butter, melted

In a small bowl, at least 1 hour before cooking, combine the first six ingredients to make the lemon sauce. Mix well, then refrigerate.

Preheat oven to 400°. Combine the flour, salt, and paprika, and coat the chicken well with the mixture.

In a shallow roasting pan, arrange the chicken pieces, skin side down, in a single layer. Brush well with butter, and bake, uncovered, for 30 minutes. Turn the chicken, and pour the sauce over it. Bake for 30 minutes longer, or until the chicken is golden brown and tender. Serves 4.

CHICKEN PICCATA

6 chicken breasts, skinned,
    split, and boned
¼ cup all-purpose flour
1 tablespoon pure olive oil
5 tablespoons sweet butter
¾ cup Kathy's Basic Chicken
    Stock (page 71)

⅓ cup lemon juice (or the
    juice of about 2 lemons)
1 teaspoon grated lemon rind
½ teaspoon salt
pepper to taste
3 tablespoons chopped
    parsley

Pound each chicken breast until thin, and then coat with the flour. In a large, heavy skillet, heat the oil and 4 tablespoons of the butter. Fry the chicken breasts on both sides until tender and lightly browned. Remove the chicken, and set aside.

To the skillet add the stock, lemon juice, lemon rind, salt, and pepper; boil for 6 minutes. Add the remaining 1 tablespoon of butter, and stir. Place the chicken back in the pan, spoon the sauce over it, and cook for an additional 2 minutes, or until heated through. Serve sprinkled with parsley. Serves 6.

CHICKEN MARRAKESH

This recipe comes from a gourmet cook whose cooking classes in Memphis, Tennessee, are very popular.

2 2½-pound chickens, quartered	2 teaspoons thyme
½ cup fresh lemon juice	1 teaspoon salt
2 tablespoons grated lemon rind	1 teaspoon pepper
1 clove garlic, peeled and crushed (optional)	¼ cup sweet butter, melted
	3 lemons, thinly sliced
	½ cup chopped parsley

Wash and dry the chicken pieces. In a shallow baking pan, arrange the chicken pieces in a single layer.

In a small bowl, combine the lemon juice, lemon rind, garlic, thyme, salt, and pepper; mix together well. Spoon this mixture over the chicken, turning to coat well. Marinate at room temperature for 3 to 4 hours, turning the chicken several times.

Preheat oven to 425°. Drain the chicken well on paper towels, reserving the marinade. In a shallow baking pan, again arrange the chicken pieces in a single layer, skin side up. Brush with the melted butter.

Bake, uncovered, for 25 minutes. Brush with the remaining marinade, and bake, covered, for 25 to 35 minutes longer, basting frequently, until the chicken is browned and cooked through. Garnish with the lemon slices, and sprinkle with chopped parsley. Serve any remaining marinade from the pan as a sauce. Serves 6 to 8.

FRIED CHICKEN HAWAIIAN

1 3-pound broiler chicken, cut up
½ cup all-purpose flour
1 teaspoon salt
¼ teaspoon pepper
¼ cup sweet butter
½ cup water

1 9-ounce can unsweetened crushed pineapple, undrained
2 teaspoons soy sauce (check the label)
Hot Rice (page 191)

Wipe the chicken well with damp paper towels. In a clean paper bag, combine the flour, salt, and pepper. Put the chicken pieces in the bag, a few pieces at a time, and shake, coating them well.

In a large skillet, heat the butter. Add half the chicken pieces, and brown well, turning often; set aside. Brown the remaining chicken. Put all the chicken back in the skillet.

In a small bowl, combine the water, pineapple, and soy sauce; pour this mixture over the chicken in the skillet. Cover. Simmer for 30 minutes, or until fork-tender. Serve over rice. Serves 4.

❁———————————————————————

BROILED CHICKEN WITH BANANAS

2 broiling chickens
  (2¼–2½ pounds each),
  halved
⅓ cup lemon juice
2 tablespoons pure vegetable
  oil
1 clove garlic, peeled and
  crushed

⅛ teaspoon nutmeg
1½ teaspoons salt
⅛ teaspoon pepper
1½ teaspoons thyme
4 small bananas
2 tablespoons honey
lemon quarters for garnish

———————————————————————

Wash the chickens, and pat dry with paper towels. Place the pieces in a large, shallow baking pan.

To make the marinade: Combine the lemon juice, oil, garlic, nutmeg, salt, pepper, and thyme, and mix together well. Pour this mixture over the chicken. Let stand at room temperature for at least 3 hours, turning several times.

Pour the marinade off, and reserve. Place the chicken, skin side down, back in the baking pan. Broil for 20 minutes, basting often with the pan juices and the reserved marinade. Turn the chicken, and broil for 15 to 20 minutes longer, basting often.

Peel and slice the bananas, and arrange the slices in the pan around the chicken. Brush the bananas with honey, and broil for 5 minutes longer. Garnish with lemon quarters, and serve. Serves 6 to 8.

CHICKEN STEW

*1 5-pound stewing chicken,
  cut up
¼ cup sweet butter
1 small onion, peeled and
  sliced*

*2 celery stalks, sliced
1 carrot, peeled and sliced
½ lemon, quartered
2 teaspoons salt
¼ cup all-purpose flour*

Wash the chicken pieces, and pat dry with paper towels. In a large kettle, heat the butter; brown the chicken pieces on both sides. Remove from heat. Add the onion, celery, carrot, lemon, and enough boiling water to cover. Bring to a boil again; reduce heat, and simmer, covered, for 45 minutes. Add the salt, and simmer, covered, for 1 hour longer, or until the chicken is tender.

Remove the kettle from the heat, and let stand until fat forms on the surface. Skim off the fat, reserving ¼ cup. Remove the chicken pieces from the broth, and place them in a warm oven. Strain the broth, reserving 3 cups.

In a saucepan, heat the reserved chicken fat; remove from heat. Gradually add the flour, stirring to make a smooth paste. Slowly add the reserved chicken broth, stirring until smooth. Return to the heat, and bring to boiling, stirring constantly. Reduce heat, and simmer for 1 minute. Spoon the sauce over the chicken, and serve. Serves 4.

CHICKEN BREASTS WITH MARMALADE

Easy, delicious, and elegant.

4 chicken breasts, split
¾ cup Basic French Dressing
   (page 224)
dash of mace

8 tablespoons ginger,
   lemon, or grapefruit
   marmalade (check the
   label)

Wash the breasts well, and marinate in the French dressing, covered, overnight in the refrigerator or for several hours at room temperature. Drain, and sprinkle with mace.

Preheat oven to 350°. Spread 1 tablespoon of the marmalade on each chicken half, and place the chicken, cut side down, in a roasting pan. Bake for 45 minutes. Before serving, pour the pan juices over the breasts. Serves 8.

⌘ CHICKEN WINGS PAULA

2 pounds chicken wings
   (about 10 wings) *
½ cup soy sauce (check
   the label)

3 tablespoons sweet butter
Sweet and Sour Sauce
   (page 153)

Cut off and discard the tips of the wings. Cut the wings at the joint into two parts. Place the pieces in a shallow bowl, and pour the soy sauce over them; cover and let stand in the refrigerator overnight.

Preheat oven to 350°. Drain the chicken wings. In a skillet, slowly heat the butter; fry the wings until browned on each side. Place in a baking pan, cover, and bake for 1 hour. Serve with Sweet and Sour Sauce on the side. Serves 4.

* To make 3 pounds of Oven-Baked Chicken Wings with Honey, substitute 3 tablespoons honey for the butter, add 2 tablespoons pure vegetable oil, and salt and pepper to taste, and pour this mixture over the wings just before baking—do not fry first. Bake for 1 hour, or until tender. Serves 6.

REALLY EASY CHICKEN LIVERS

1 pound chicken livers
¼ cup pure vegetable oil
¼ cup Cleo Jeppson's
  Bread Crumbs (page 262)

½ teaspoon salt
dash of pepper

Preheat oven to 350°. Dip the livers in the oil. Combine the bread crumbs with the salt and pepper, and then roll the livers in the seasoned bread crumbs. Place on a baking sheet, and bake for 15 to 20 minutes. Serves 4.

CHICKEN SALAD SPREAD

Use this as a sandwich spread for lunches, or spread it on toasted rounds for an appetizer.

1 cup chopped cooked
  chicken
¼ cup chopped walnuts
¼ cup chopped water
  chestnuts

2 tablespoons chopped celery
2 tablespoons homemade
  mayonnaise
  (page 223)

In a medium bowl, combine all the ingredients, and beat until smooth.

CHINESE CHICKEN SALAD FOR TWENTY

Judy of Santa Clara, California, shares this recipe, which can be served with or without dressing.

8 pounds turkey or chicken breasts
1 cup canned hoisin sauce (check the label)
pure vegetable oil for frying
1 head lettuce, shredded
½ pound Chinese rice noodles (check the label)
4 stalks celery, chopped
1 bunch green onions, including the tops, chopped
¼ cup sesame seeds, toasted
¾ teaspoon dry mustard
1 clove garlic, peeled and pressed (optional)
¼ cup pure vegetable oil
½ cup soy sauce (check the label)
1 teaspoon sugar
¾ teaspoon ground ginger
2 tablespoons lemon juice

Brush the turkey or chicken breasts heavily with the hoisin sauce; roast in a covered roasting pan for about 45 minutes at 350°. Let cool enough to cut into julienne strips.

In a skillet, slowly heat ½ inch oil. Drop small amounts of the noodles into the hot oil—they should puff immediately. Remove at once with a slotted spoon—do not brown.

In a large bowl, combine the turkey or chicken, lettuce, celery, and green onions. Top with noodles and sesame seeds. In a separate bowl, combine the remaining ingredients. Pour this dressing over the salad and serve at once. Serves 20.

SYBIL'S HEAVENLY CHICKEN

This recipe from Alabama is a good way to use up turkey or chicken after holiday dinners.

1 10-ounce package frozen broccoli, cooked
½ cup grated white Swiss cheese
4 slices cooked turkey or chicken
1 cup White Sauce for Heavenly Chicken (page 150)
dash of nutmeg
1 tablespoon homemade mayonnaise (page 223)

Preheat oven to 325°. Grease a baking dish. In the bottom of the baking dish, arrange the broccoli and add half the grated cheese. Top with the turkey or chicken slices.

In a small bowl, mix the white sauce, nutmeg, and mayonnaise. Pour this over the broccoli, cheese, and meat mixture. Sprinkle the remaining cheese on top. Bake for 20 minutes, then put under the broiler for 5 minutes to brown. Serves 4.

SUSAN'S CRUSTY COATING MIX

This recipe for a homemade chicken coating comes from Houston. It can also be used on fish filets or pork chops. This amount is enough for six boned chicken breasts or two cut-up fryers.

1 cup wheat germ
1 cup whole-wheat flour
1 heaping teaspoon chopped parsley

¼ teaspoon oregano
salt to taste
¼ teaspoon black pepper

Preheat oven to 400°. Lightly grease a large, shallow baking pan. Wash the chicken pieces under cold water, and pat dry with paper towels. Salt the pieces. In a clean plastic or paper bag, combine the coating ingredients; twist the bag to close it, and shake to mix the ingredients well. Add the chicken pieces, one at a time, to the bag; tie the bag, and shake to coat well. Arrange the chicken on a baking sheet. Bake for 50 minutes, or until the chicken is fork-tender and golden brown. Makes about 2 cups.

CORNISH HENS, BROILED

2 Cornish hens, halved
½ teaspoon salt

4 tablespoons sweet butter, softened

Season the hens with the salt, and rub them with 2 tablespoons of the butter. Place the hens, skin side down, in a broiling pan on the lowest broiler rack in the oven. Broil for 20 minutes. Turn, baste with the remaining 2 tablespoons butter, and broil for 15 to 20 minutes longer, or until the skin is crisped and brown. Serves 4.

✣————————————

ROAST TURKEY

Never use self-basting turkeys—they contain artificial color in the basting liquid. The pan juices of the roasted turkey make excellent gravy.

1 turkey, thawed, if frozen	*Italian Stuffing Lynn*
2 tablespoons salt	*(page 99)*
1 teaspoon pepper	*¼ pound sweet butter or*
1 teaspoon paprika	*melted chicken fat*
½ teaspoon ground ginger	

The day before serving, wash and clean the turkey well. In a small bowl, mix together all the spices. Rub the turkey inside and out with the seasonings. Refrigerate for at least 12 hours.

Preheat oven to 350°. Stuff the turkey, and rub ½ of the melted butter or chicken fat over its entire skin surface. Place on a rack in an open baking pan, breast side down. Cover well with a double thickness of cheesecloth, tucking in the ends around the legs and wings. Add 1 cup of hot water to the pan, and roast for 15 to 30 minutes per pound, or until the back is well browned. Turn breast side up, cover again with the cheesecloth, and continue cooking. (When the legs move easily, the turkey is done.) For the last 20 minutes of cooking, remove the cheesecloth, brush with butter or chicken fat, and let the skin brown and become crisp. (Additional hot water may be added as the water in pan cooks down.) Let the turkey stand for 15 minutes on the platter before carving.

✂—————————————
TURKEY, THE DAY AFTER

4 tablespoons sweet butter
1 large onion, peeled and
  sliced
1 cup sliced celery, cut on
  the diagonal
½ pound fresh mushrooms,
  sliced

1 8-ounce can water
  chestnuts, drained and
  sliced
2 cups diced cooked turkey

WHITE SAUCE:

3 tablespoons sweet butter
3 tablespoons all-purpose
  flour
1¼ cups milk or Kathy's
  Basic Chicken Stock
  (page 71) or canned
  broth (check the label)

salt and pepper to taste
dash of lemon juice
2 cups cooked Chinese
  noodles (check the label)

In a skillet, slowly heat the butter; sauté the onion, celery, and mushrooms for a few minutes until the onions are transparent. Stir in the water chestnuts and turkey; set aside.

To make the white sauce: in a saucepan, melt the butter. Gradually add the flour, mixing well. Slowly stir in the milk or chicken stock. Cook over medium heat, stirring constantly, for a few minutes, or until the sauce thickens. Season with the salt and pepper and the lemon juice.

Pour the white sauce over the turkey mixture, and heat well. Serve over the Chinese noodles. Serves 2.

CRISPY DUCK

1 duck, halved
½ teaspoon salt
½ teaspoon ground ginger

Sweet-Sour Sauce for Duck
(below), optional

Preheat an electric frying pan to 350°, or heat a heavy skillet. Rub the seasonings into the duck very well. Put the duck, skin side down, in a skillet, and cook, covered, for 20 minutes. Turn to the other side, and cook, covered, for 20 minutes. Turn to skin side down again, and cook for another 20 minutes. (Total cooking time: 1 hour.) Skin should be very crisp. Serve with plain rice and, if desired, Sweet-Sour Sauce for Duck. Serves 4.

SWEET-SOUR SAUCE FOR DUCK

2 tablespoons duck fat
2 tablespoons all-purpose
   flour
½ cup Kathy's Basic
   Chicken Stock (page 71)
   or canned broth (check
   the label)

1 tablespoon soy sauce
   (check the label)
1 8½ ounce can
   unsweetened pineapple
   chunks, drained

Over medium heat in a small skillet, melt the fat. Add the flour, and stir until bubbly. Gradually stir in the chicken stock and soy sauce, stirring constantly until the sauce thickens. Add the pineapple chunks, and cook just until heated. Serve with Crispy Duck (above). Makes ¾ cup.

ITALIAN STUFFING LYNN

Served with turkey or chicken, this is a stuffing with a different flavor. It will stuff a fifteen-pound turkey or two large roasting chickens.

½ pound sweet butter
2 cups peeled and chopped onions
3 cups finely chopped celery
1½ pounds small, fresh mushrooms
1 pound pure pork sausage meat (check the label)
1 teaspoon chopped parsley
1 teaspoon oregano
1 teaspoon peeled and finely minced onion
1½ loaves cubed white bread

In a large skillet, melt the butter. Sauté the chopped onions, celery, mushrooms, and sausage until the sausage is well cooked, about 15 to 20 minutes. Stir in the parsley, oregano, and minced onion; remove from heat, and let cool. When cool, add the bread cubes; toss to mix well.

MEAT

SUSIE'S ROAST BEEF SUPREME

If you prefer your beef medium-rare, this is a perfect dish for you, and so easy to prepare. It is dark and crisp outside and pink inside, and its drippings can be used for gravy or Yorkshire pudding.

1 4-pound two-rib roast

Seasoned Salt (page 159) or salt and pepper to taste

Preheat oven to 500°. Season the roast with salt and pepper or seasoned salt, and place it on a rack in a roasting pan. Cook on the next-to-bottom shelf of the oven for 20 minutes (5 minutes per pound). At the end of that time turn the oven off, and LEAVE THE DOOR CLOSED for 2 hours—no peeking! Serves 6.

JAPANESE POT ROAST

1 4-pound chuck roast, 2 inches thick
¼ cup all-purpose flour
2 tablespoons pure vegetable oil

⅓ cup soy sauce (check the label)
1 cup water
1 medium onion, peeled and sliced

Rub the roast well with flour to coat, reserving any remaining flour. In a dutch oven or large skillet, heat the oil; brown the roast on all sides slowly over medium heat for 20 minutes.

In a medium bowl, combine the soy sauce with the water; stir to mix. Pour this over the beef. Add the onion to the skillet, cover, and simmer for about 2 hours, or until the beef is tender. Remove to a serving platter.

In a small bowl, mix the remaining flour with enough cold water to make a smooth paste. Gradually stir this into the pan drippings. Cook over low heat, stirring, until the gravy is thickened. Serve with the roast. Serve 4 to 6.

BEEF STROGANOFF

Leftover roast beef can be used for this recipe.

2 tablespoons pure vegetable oil
2½ pounds round steak, cut into thin strips against the grain
1 onion, peeled and finely chopped
1 clove garlic, peeled and chopped (optional)
1 cup Kathy's Basic Beef Stock (page 71) or canned broth (check the label)
1 cup commercial sour cream

In a large skillet, heat the oil; brown the meat and onions. Add the garlic and beef stock, cover, and simmer until the beef is tender—if round steak, 35 minutes; if leftover beef, 15 minutes.

Just before serving add the sour cream and stir just until heated through. Serves 4 to 6.

BAKED FRESH BEEF BRISKET

1 5-pound beef brisket
2 yellow onions, peeled and thinly sliced
salt and pepper to taste

Preheat oven to 300°.

In a dutch oven or skillet, brown the brisket and onions over medium heat for about 20 minutes, seasoning with salt and pepper. Cover, and bake for at least 3 hours, adding ¼ cup of water, if necessary, at the end of the baking time. To serve, cut on the diagonal, against the grain. Serves 6.

⌘─────────────────────

CORNED BEEF HASH PUFFS

1 16-ounce can corned beef hash (check the label)
2 eggs, separated

½ teaspoon salt
8 sprigs parsley, finely chopped

Grease a baking sheet. In a medium bowl, break up the hash with a fork. In a separate bowl, beat the yolks of the eggs until they are thick and very light in color. Add the yolks, salt, and parsley to the hash; mix thoroughly.

In another bowl, beat the egg whites at high speed until very stiff; gently fold them into the mixture. Drop 8 mounds of the mixture onto a baking sheet. Broil for 10 minutes, or until baked through and brown on top. Serves 4.

PALUSAMI

This is a Fijian dish that is delicious and has a most unusual, delectable sauce. This recipe has been adapted to the ingredients in our markets.

1 pound fresh spinach, well washed
1 12-ounce can corned beef (check the label) or leftover corned beef, sliced
1 onion, peeled and chopped
½ can beets, drained and finely diced
1 cup commercial or homemade coconut milk (page 152)

Preheat oven to 350°. In a large baking dish or casserole, layer half the spinach leaves on the bottom. Cover with half the slices of corned beef, half the onion, and half the beets. Repeat the layers. Pour the coconut milk over all. Bake for 30 minutes. Serves 4.

SYRIL'S PASTRAMI

Here is another variation on corned beef, which takes time but is well worth the effort. Save the cooking liquid for cooking lentils, yellow or green split peas, cabbage, or for soup made with these vegetables.

1 5-pound corned-beef, center-cut brisket
1 onion, peeled and sliced
1 tablespoon ground allspice
1 tablespoon coarsely ground black pepper
paprika

In a large pot, cover the corned beef with cold water; bring to a boil over moderate heat. Pour off the water so that the meat will not be too salty, and cover again with cold water. Add the onion slices, and bring to a boil again over moderate heat. Reduce heat, and simmer for 2 hours, or until partially tender.

Preheat oven to 350°. Drain the corned beef, reserving the liquid, and place the meat in a roasting pan. Cover the top of the meat completely with spices. Pour in 2 cups of the reserved liquid, cover, and bake for 1 hour, or until the meat is tender. Serves 4 to 6.

✂——————————————————————
BRENDA'S BEEF GOULASH

3 tablespoons sweet butter
3 cups peeled and thinly
   sliced onions
3 pounds boneless beef
   chuck, cut into 1½-inch
   cubes

1 tablespoon paprika
salt to taste
1 8-ounce package wide
   noodles (check the label)
2 tablespoons poppy seeds
1 cup water

In a heavy skillet, heat the butter. Add the onions, and cook for 2 minutes.

Season the meat with the paprika and salt. Add the meat to the skillet, and cook, uncovered, for 20 minutes, over medium heat or until the liquid that the meat gives off cooks down. Add the water, cover, and cook over low heat for 2 hours, or until the meat is tender, checking occasionally, and if necessary, adding additional water.

Cook the noodles according to package directions, until tender. Drain. Sprinkle with the poppy seeds. Pour the beef mixture over the noodles. Serves 6.

❦ PINEAPPLE STEAK

1 2-pound round steak, 1–2
   inches thick
¼ cup all-purpose flour
2 teaspoons salt
pepper to taste
¼ cup pure vegetable oil
2 large onions, peeled and
   sliced

1¼ cups pineapple juice
1 8-ounce can unsweetened
   pineapple chunks, drained
   (save the juice)
2 tablespoons chopped
   parsley

Sprinkle the steak on both sides with flour, salt, and pepper. With a mallet, pound the steak until all the flour disappears. Cut into 8 pieces.

In a large skillet over medium heat, heat the oil. Add the steak and brown well on each side for approximately 10 minutes. Add the onions and pineapple juice. Reduce heat to low, cover, and simmer for 50 to 55 minutes, stirring occasionally, until the meat is tender. Add the pineapple chunks, and cook until heated through. Place on a heated serving platter, and sprinkle with parsley. Serves 4 to 6.

❦ FLANK STEAK

Great for a barbecue grill, and it's so easy to prepare.

1 1–1½-pound flank steak,
   in one piece

½ cup soy sauce (check the
   label)

At least 6 hours before serving, pour enough of the soy sauce over the steak to cover, and let stand all day. Drain. Broil in the oven for 5 minutes on one side. Turn the meat, and broil for 3 minutes longer for rare steak, 5 minutes for medium. To serve, slice diagonally in very thin slices. Serves 4 to 6.

✂ ───────────────────
STIR-FRY STRAGONI

1 1½-pound round steak
½ cup plus 2 tablespoons
 soy sauce (check the label)
1 onion, peeled and finely
 chopped
2 tablespoons pure vegetable
 oil
½ cup finely chopped celery
1 cup finely chopped zucchini

1 cup peeled and finely
 chopped carrots
1 cup finely chopped
 mushrooms
1 tablespoon all-purpose
 flour
½ teaspoon ground ginger
Hot Rice (page 191)

With a sharp knife, cut the round steak into narrow strips.
In a shallow bowl, combine ½ cup of the soy sauce and the
onion, and marinate the steak for 1 hour.

In a large skillet, heat the oil and stir-fry the chopped
vegetables with the remaining 2 tablespoons soy sauce over
high heat. Add the meat and marinade, and stir-fry until the
meat is done. Remove the meat to a serving platter, and keep
warm.

In a small cup, combine the flour, ginger, and 2 tablespoons water; pour this into the pan juices, and stir until
thickened. Serve the meat and gravy with hot rice. Serves
4 to 6.

✂ ───────────────────
BEEF WITH SNOW PEAS

1 1½-pound flank steak
4 tablespoons pure peanut oil
½ pound fresh snow peas or
 1 10-ounce package frozen
 snow peas, thawed and
 drained

2 thin slices peeled fresh
 ginger or ¼ teaspoon
 ground ginger
5 green onions, including
 the tops, sliced
Hot Rice (page 191)

MARINADE:

3 tablespoons soy sauce　　*1 tablespoon cornstarch*
　(check the label)

SAUCE:

1 tablespoon soy sauce　　*1 teaspoon sugar*
　(check the label)　　　*2 tablespoons water*

Cut the steak lengthwise into 2½-by-3-inch strips, trimming off all fat; then cut across the grain in ¼-inch-thick strips.

In a shallow dish, mix together the marinade ingredients. Toss the meat in the mixture to coat, and marinate at room temperature for at least 30 minutes. Meanwhile, in a small bowl, combine the sauce ingredients; set aside.

In a wok or large skillet, heat 2 tablespoons of the oil. Add the snow peas, and cook, stirring constantly, for about 1 minute. Remove the snow peas to a serving plate. Add the 2 remaining tablespoons oil to the pan; brown the ginger. Stir in the green onions and beef; cook for about 3 minutes. Return the snow peas to the pan. Pour the sauce over the mixture, and stir for 1 additional minute. Serve over rice. Serves 4 to 6.

SWEET AND SOUR MEAT BALLS

1 *pound ground beef*
1 *egg*
salt to taste
¼ *cup matzo meal*
1 *20-ounce can unsweetened chunk pineapple*
1 *cup Kathy's Basic Chicken Stock (page 71) or canned broth (check the label)*

2 *tablespoons cornstarch*
2 *teaspoons soy sauce (check the label)*
¼ *cup brown sugar*
1 *cup sliced celery*
1 *medium onion, peeled and sliced*
½ *carrot, peeled and sliced*
Hot Rice (page 191)

In a large bowl, combine the ground beef, egg, salt, and matzo meal; mix together well. Shape into small meat balls.

Drain the canned pineapple, reserving 1 cup of the liquid. In a medium bowl, combine the reserved pineapple liquid, chicken stock, cornstarch, soy sauce, and brown sugar, stirring to blend well. In a large skillet, brown the meat balls on all sides over medium heat. Add the pineapple, celery, onion, and carrot. Pour the sauce over the meat ball mixture in the skillet. Bring the mixture to a boil; lower heat, cover, and simmer for 15 minutes. Serve over hot rice. Serves 4.

MEAT LOAF

The hard-boiled eggs make the loaf more attractive when serving.

1 pound ground round
1 onion, peeled and finely chopped
1 egg, slightly beaten
2 tablespoons Cleo Jeppson's Bread Crumbs (page 262) or matzo meal
1 teaspoon salt
1 teaspoon chopped parsley
½ teaspoon pepper
½ teaspoon soy sauce, optional (check the label)
3 hard-boiled eggs

Preheat oven to 350°. Grease a loaf pan.

In a large bowl, mix together all the ingredients except the hard-boiled eggs. Press a third of the mixture evenly into the loaf pan. Arrange the whole shelled hard-boiled eggs lengthwise down the center of the mixture. Gently cover them with the remaining meat mixture, and pat down. Bake for 1 hour. Serves 4 to 6.

VEAL AND MUSHROOM LOAF

3 pounds ground veal
2 tablespoons sweet butter
1 cup peeled and finely chopped onion
1 cup finely chopped celery
1 pound mushrooms, thinly sliced
1 cup Cleo Jeppson's Bread Crumbs (page 262)
1 cup chopped parsley (or cut with kitchen shears)
2 eggs
salt and pepper to taste

Preheat oven to 375°. Grease a loaf pan. In a skillet, melt the butter; add the onion and celery, and cook briefly over low heat, until the onion wilts. Add the mushrooms, and cook until the liquid they give off evaporates. Let cool.

Place the veal in a bowl, and pour the vegetable mixture over it. Add the remaining ingredients, and mix together well. Press the mixture evenly into the loaf pan. Place the pan in a larger baking dish, and pour about 1½ inches of boiling water into the baking dish. Bake for 1 to 1¼ hours. Serve either hot or cold. Serves 8.

PATTI'S HAMBURGER CHOW MEIN

What a great combination—hamburger and chow mein!

1 pound ground beef
3 tablespoons pure vegetable oil
½ cup chopped celery
1 cup fresh mushrooms, sliced
½ cup chopped green onion, including the tops
1 tablespoon cornstarch
1 cup Kathy's Basic Beef Stock (page 71) or canned broth (check the label)
2 tablespoons soy sauce (check the label)
chow mein noodles (check the label)

In a wok or large skillet, brown the meat, turning frequently and watching that it doesn't stick. Remove the meat from the pan, and set aside. Add the oil to the pan, and, with a fork, stir-fry the celery, mushrooms, and onions until tender—about 5 minutes. Combine with the meat.

In a small bowl, dissolve the cornstarch in the beef stock and soy sauce. Pour this sauce into the skillet, and cook, stirring, over low heat until thickened and hot. Add the meat mixture, and cook, stirring, until warm.

Heat the chow mein noodles in the oven, according to package directions, and serve with the meat mixture. Serves 4.

✂ JOANN'S VERSION OF JOE'S SPECIAL

Even children who think they don't like spinach will love this.

3 tablespoons pure olive oil
1 small onion, peeled and
   chopped
½ clove garlic, peeled and
   chopped
1½ pounds ground beef
1 package frozen chopped
   spinach, cooked

4 eggs, slightly beaten
salt and pepper to taste
1 12-ounce package medium
   noodles, cooked (check
   the label)
2 tablespoons sweet butter

In a skillet, heat the olive oil. Add the onion, garlic, and beef, and pan-fry until browned. Add the cooked spinach, and cook, stirring, until hot. Pour in the eggs, and cook, stirring, until set. Season with salt and pepper. Serve over buttered cooked noodles. Serves 6.

HAMBURGER-POTATO PIE

This is a delicious variation of the ever-popular hamburger.

1 pound ground round
salt and pepper to taste
1 small onion, peeled and chopped
2 cups Mashed Potatoes (page 173)
¼ cup grated white cheese

Preheat oven to 350°. In a medium bowl, season the meat with salt and pepper. Add the onion, and mix together well. Press the mixture into a pie plate. Bake just until browned—about 15 to 20 minutes.

Drain off the excess fat. Spread the mashed potatoes on top. Bake for about 30 minutes longer. Sprinkle grated cheese over the top, and bake just until the cheese is melted. Serves 4 to 6.

BURRITOS

If wrapped well in foil and heavy paper, these will stay warm in lunch boxes.

1 16-ounce can refried beans (check the label)
1 onion, peeled and chopped
½ pound ground beef, cooked
¼ pound white Cheddar cheese, grated or shredded
4 to 8 flour tortillas (check the label)
pure vegetable oil for frying

In a medium bowl, mix all the ingredients together except for the oil and tortillas. Place about 2 tablespoons of the mixture in the center of each tortilla; fold the tortilla over like a baby's diaper.

In a large skillet, heat a small amount of oil. Fry the stuffed tortillas on both sides (must be crisp on both sides), until heated through. Serves 4.

✿ DINNER-IN-A-DISH

8 ounce package egg noodles (check the label)
1 quart water
1½ pounds ground beef
1 small onion, peeled and finely chopped
1 cup peeled and diced carrots

1 cup canned peas, drained
1 teaspoon salt
¼ teaspoon pepper
2 tablespoons Cleo Jeppson's Bread Crumbs (page 262)
3 tablespoons sweet butter

Preheat oven to 350°. Cook the noodles according to package directions; drain and set aside.

In a skillet, brown the beef; add the water, the onion, and the carrots, and cook until the carrots are tender—about 5 minutes. Stir in the noodles, and add the peas, salt, and pepper; mix together well. Pour into a casserole dish. Sprinkle with the bread crumbs and bits of butter. Bake for 30 minutes, or until golden brown. Serves 6 to 8.

✿ JEANNIE'S SUPPER ON FRENCH BREAD

Great for potlucks or parents' groups as well as for the children.

1 loaf French bread	¾ cup peeled and chopped
2 pounds ground beef	onion
1 can evaporated skimmed	1⅓ tablespoons homemade
milk	mustard (page 158)
¾ cup Cleo Jeppson's Bread	2 teaspoons salt
Crumbs (page 262) or	pepper to taste
matzo meal	2½ cups grated white
	Cheddar cheese

Preheat oven to 350°. Cut the French bread in half lengthwise. Mix all the remaining ingredients together except for the cheese. Spread this mixture evenly on both halves of the bread. Wrap aluminum foil around each crust, but do not cover the meat, only the bread crust and the sides of the meat. Cover the top of each half loaf with grated cheese. Place on a baking sheet, and bake for 35 to 40 minutes. Cut into 2-inch slices to make 20 to 25 pieces.

⌘————————————————————————

GERRIE'S FAVORITE CASSEROLE

7 tablespoons sweet butter	3 cups peeled and diced
1½ pounds ground beef	potatoes
1 large onion, peeled and	3 tablespoons all-purpose
diced	flour
2 cups peeled and diced	1½ teaspoons salt
carrots	¼ teaspoon pepper
	2 cups milk

Preheat oven to 350°. Grease a casserole dish with 4 tablespoons of the butter. In a large skillet, melt the remaining 3 tablespoons butter. Brown the ground beef and onion lightly.

Stir in the carrots and potatoes. Pour the mixture into the casserole.

Place the flour, salt, and pepper in a medium saucepan, and gradually stir in the milk. Cook over low heat until slightly thickened. Pour this sauce over the beef mixture, and bake for 1½ hours, or until the potatoes are tender. Serves 6 to 8.

❦————————————————————————

CHURCH SUPPER MEAT LOAF

To make this a distinctive and attractive meat loaf, try adding hard-boiled eggs to the center of the loaf. Press a third of the meat into the pans, lay in 3 or 4 whole eggs lengthwise in each pan, and cover with the remaining meat. When the loaf is sliced, the center is a pretty surprise.

6 pounds ground beef
2 pounds ground pork
3 teaspoons salt
4 large onions, peeled and
   finely chopped

4 cups Cleo Jeppson's Bread
   Crumbs (page 262)
2 cups water
1 teaspoon pepper
1 teaspoon dry mustard

Preheat oven to 375°. Grease 4 loaf pans. In a very large bowl, combine all the ingredients. Turn the mixture into the loaf pans. Bake for 45 minutes. Serves 24.

❦————————————————————————

MOCK HOT DOGS

The children in the family will think these are a great treat.

¼ teaspoon paprika
¼ cup wheat germ
2 tablespoons nutritional (Brewer's) yeast
1½ pounds ground meat
2 eggs, slightly beaten
1 onion, peeled and grated

1 large carrot, peeled and grated
1 clove garlic, peeled and minced
pinches of oregano, marjoram, and thyme

In a small bowl, mix together the paprika, wheat germ, and yeast; set aside. In a large bowl, thoroughly mix the rest of the ingredients. Shape into 6 hot dogs. Roll each one in the wheat germ mixture. Place in a baking pan, and broil on a broiler rack on all sides until done—15 to 20 minutes. **Serves 6.**

SPARERIBS FOR FEINGOLDERS

Choose lean but meaty ribs, and be sure that they can be cut through. Serve this dish with a bean casserole or Tanya's Sweet Potato Tzimmes (page 184).

10 ribs in one piece
2 tablespoons soy sauce (check the label)

2 tablespoons honey or pure maple syrup
¼ cup hot water

Preheat oven to 325°.

Rub each side of the ribs well with the soy sauce. Place them in a roasting pan, and pour the honey or syrup over them. Bake, covered, for 45 minutes. Turn the ribs, and add the water if necessary. Bake for 45 minutes longer, checking to see if more liquid is needed. When done, cut into portions of 2 to 3 ribs for serving. Serves 2 generously.

❦————————————————————

SPARERIBS WITH SAUERKRAUT

This is a German style of preparing this cut.

8 spareribs, cut into 4 pieces	1 teaspoon caraway seeds
1 27-ounce can sauerkraut	pepper to taste
1 small potato, peeled and grated	¼ cup hot water

In a pre-heated, 3-quart dutch oven, brown the meat well on both sides over medium heat. Add the remaining ingredients, cover tightly, reduce heat to low, and cook for 2 hours, or until the meat is tender. Serves 4.

SWEET-SOUR PORK

This recipe has been a Feingold family favorite for years.

1 egg, slightly beaten	dash of pepper
1 tablespoon pure olive oil	1 small clove garlic, peeled and finely minced
2 pounds pork, cut into cubes	5 tablespoons sugar
6 tablespoons cornstarch or all-purpose flour	2 cups pure vegetable oil for deep frying
3 carrots, peeled and sliced diagonally	1 7¾-ounce can unsweetened pineapple chunks, drained, reserving the liquid
¼ cup white distilled vinegar	
½ cup water or reserved pineapple juice	½ teaspoon unsulphured Chinese bead molasses (optional) (check the label)
1½ teaspoons soy sauce (check the label)	

In a bowl, beat the egg with the olive oil. Dip the pork cubes in 5 tablespoons of the cornstarch, then in the egg-oil mixture, and then again in the cornstarch. Set aside.

In a saucepan, cook the carrots in a small amount of boiling salted water for 1 minute. In a separate bowl, make the sweet-sour sauce: Mix together the vinegar, water or pineapple juice, soy sauce, pepper, garlic, and sugar. Set aside.

In a deep skillet, slowly heat the vegetable oil. Fry the pork cubes until browned; drain on paper towels.

In a small bowl, mix the remaining 1 tablespoon cornstarch with 1 tablespoon of water. In a skillet over high heat, bring the sweet-sour sauce to a boil; add the cornstarch mixture, and stir until the gravy thickens. Add the cooked carrots and the canned pineapple, and stir. Quickly stir in the pork and Chinese bead molasses, continuing to stir until all is well coated. Serves 4.

❦————————————————————————

PORK CHOPS HAWAIIAN

6 loin pork chops
salt and pepper to taste
3 tablespoons all-purpose
   flour
1 tablespoon pure peanut oil
6 slices fresh or
   canned pineapple

6 small carrots, peeled
½ cup water
1 tablespoon Wondra flour
1 teaspoon soy sauce
   (check the label)

Wipe the pork chops with paper towels. Sprinkle with salt and pepper, and dust with the flour.

In a skillet, heat the oil; add the chops, and brown over medium heat on both sides. Place a slice of pineapple on each chop, and arrange the carrots between the chops. Add the water, cover, and cook over low heat for 1½ hours, adding more water if necessary.

When done, remove the chops to a serving platter. Shake the Wondra flour into the pan juices, and cook, stirring, until thickened. Add soy sauce, and serve over the chops. Serves 6.

⚘————————————————

JOSH'S PORK CHOPS

1 cup Susan's Crusty Coating Mix (page 94)	1 tablespoon pure olive oil
	6 pork chops
1 egg, slightly beaten	salt and pepper to taste

Preheat oven to 350°. Grease a baking pan.

In a medium bowl, beat together the egg and oil. Pour the coating mix into a plastic bag. Shake each chop in the coating, then dip in the beaten egg, then shake again in the coating. Arrange the chops in the baking pan, and bake for 45 minutes or until fork-tender. Serves 4 to 6.

⚘————————————————

ROAST LEG OF LAMB WITH ARTICHOKES

This takes time to prepare but is well worth the effort. Vegetables and meat will be ready at the same time—and in one cooking pan. It's an excellent company dinner.

1 leg of lamb, about 5 pounds	½ teaspoon oregano
rind of 1 small lemon	3 artichokes
1 clove garlic, peeled and slivered	¼ cup fresh lemon juice
	6 new potatoes
1 tablespoon dried dillweed	¼ cup water
1 teaspoon salt	

Preheat oven to 425°. Remove the skin and as much fat as possible from the leg of lamb. Place the lamb, fat side up, in a large, shallow roasting pan.

Cut the lemon rind into slivers. Make small slits with a paring knife over the surface of the lamb. Roll the lemon rind and garlic slivers in the dillweed, and insert slivers into each slit; reserve any remaining dillweed. Sprinkle the meat with the salt and oregano. Roast in the oven for 15 minutes, then lower the heat to 325°, and roast for 30 minutes longer.

Meanwhile, trim the stalks from the bases of the artichokes, cut a slice from the tops, and snip off the spiky ends from the remaining leaves. Parboil or steam the artichokes until half done—about 15 minutes. Drain well. When cool, cut in half lengthwise, remove the chokes, and rub all the cut surfaces with lemon juice.

Wash the potatoes and pare a ring of peel from around the middle of each. Parboil for 5 minutes, and drain well.

When the lamb has cooked for 45 minutes, add the artichokes and potatoes to the pan. Combine the remaining lemon juice with the water and the remaining dillweed, and drizzle this over the lamb and vegetables. Roast for 45 minutes longer for rarer lamb, 1 hour longer for more well-done lamb. Serves 6.

⌘———————————

LAMB KEBABS

½ cup white distilled
   vinegar
¼ cup soy sauce
   (check the label)
2 tablespoons pure olive oil

2 teaspoons peeled and
   chopped onion
salt and pepper to taste
1½ pounds lamb,
   cut into 2-inch cubes

At least 3 hours before serving, in a saucepan, combine the vinegar, soy sauce, oil, onion, and salt and pepper; bring to a boil. Let cool thoroughly. Stir in the lamb cubes, and marinate for 2 to 3 hours.

Drain the lamb, reserving the liquid. Arrange the lamb on skewers; brush with the marinade. Broil on a barbecue or grill to the desired degree of doneness, brushing with the marinade. Serves 4.

⌘————————————

LAMB PATTIES

2 pounds ground lamb
½ cup wheat germ
3 eggs, slightly beaten

1 teaspoon homemade
mustard (page 158)
salt and pepper to taste

In a medium bowl, combine all the ingredients. Shape into patties, and place in a pan on the broiler rack of the oven, or on a barbecue grill. Broil on both sides until pink. Serves 4 to 6.

⌘————————————

LEMONY LAMB SHANKS

5 tablespoons all-purpose
flour
1 teaspoon salt
pepper to taste
½ teaspoon paprika
4 lamb shanks

2 tablespoons solid Crisco
shortening
3 tablespoons grated lemon
rind
½ cup lemon juice
1¾ cup water

In a medium bowl, combine 4 tablespoons of the flour with the salt, pepper, and paprika; dip each lamb shank in the flour mixture to coat.

In a dutch oven or heavy skillet, slowly heat the shortening. Brown the lamb shanks on all sides. Add 1½ cups of the water, the lemon rind, and the lemon juice, and bring to a boil. Reduce heat, cover, and simmer slowly for 1½ to 2 hours, or until the lamb is tender. Transfer the shanks to a plate, and keep warm in the oven.

Skim the fat from the pan liquids. Blend in the remaining 1 tablespoon flour plus ¼ cup of water; cook, stirring, until the gravy thickens. Pour over the shanks, and serve. Serves 4.

LEG OF LAMB ITALIENNE

Have the butcher butterfly the leg of lamb, and save the bones to make barley soup.

1 5-pound leg of lamb
1 teaspoon garlic salt
1 teaspoon onion salt

2 teaspoons mixed Italian
seasonings

The day before serving, rub the inside of the lamb leg well with the seasonings. Tie, and let stand overnight in the refrigerator.

Preheat oven to 350°. Roast the leg of lamb for 1 hour for pinker lamb, 1½ hours for more well-done lamb. Serves 6.

%———————————————————

BREADED VEAL WITH LEMON

After breading meats, place them in the refrigerator for an hour before cooking. That way the coating will adhere to the meat better.

*4 thin veal cutlets,
    about ¼ pound each
salt and freshly ground
    pepper to taste
2 eggs
3 tablespoons water
1 tablespoon pure olive oil*

*all-purpose flour for
    dredging
1 cup Cleo Jeppson's Bread
    Crumbs (page 262)
½ cup pure peanut oil
4 thin slices lemon, seeded*

Place each cutlet between sheets of plastic wrap, and pound with a flat mallet or the bottom of a heavy skillet until thin. Sprinkle the meat on both sides with salt and pepper.

In a small bowl, beat the eggs with the water. Add the olive oil, mix well, and set aside. Coat the veal on both sides with flour. Dip each slice in the egg mixture and then in the bread crumbs until uniformly coated.

In a large skillet, heat half the peanut oil. Cook the veal over medium heat until nicely browned on each side, adding more oil if necessary. Serve on hot plates with a lemon slice on each piece. Serves 2.

❀
VEAL PAPRIKA

½ teaspoon salt
1 cup plus 1 tablespoon
  all-purpose flour
2 pounds veal cutlets,
  each ¼ inch thick
½ cup pure vegetable oil
1 cup peeled and
  diced onion
1½ teaspoons paprika

½ cup Kathy's Basic Chicken
  Stock (page 71) or
  canned broth (check the
  label)
1 tablespoon cornstarch
1 cup plain, additive-free
  yogurt
chopped parsley for garnish

In a medium bowl, mix the salt with 1 cup of the flour. Dip the cutlets into the flour mixture, and shake off the excess. In a large skillet, heat the oil. Lightly sauté the cutlets over medium heat until browned—approximately 3 to 4 minutes on each side. Place in a baking dish, and set aside.

In the same skillet, sauté the onion over medium heat until golden brown. Add the paprika, the chicken stock, the remaining 1 tablespoon flour, the cornstarch, and the yogurt, and stir constantly until the mixture is smooth. Heat for 5 minutes over low heat, stirring occasionally. Return the cutlets to the sauce, and heat for an additional 5 minutes. Garnish with parsley. Serves 6.

VEAL PAPRIKA WITH NOODLES

2 pounds boned veal
shoulder, cubed
3 tablespoons all-purpose
flour
4 tablespoons sweet butter
¼ cup peeled and
chopped onion
1 cup Kathy's Basic
Chicken Stock (page 71)
or canned broth (check
the label)

½ teaspoon salt
pepper to taste
1 tablespoon sesame seeds
1 8-ounce package medium
noodles (check the label)
2 teaspoons paprika
¾ cup commercial sour
cream or plain, additive-
free yogurt

Coat the veal cubes with the flour. In a heavy skillet or dutch oven, slowly heat 2 tablespoons of the butter; brown the veal on all sides. Add the onions, and cook, stirring, until tender—3 to 5 minutes. Add the chicken stock, salt, and pepper. Bring to a boil; cover, reduce heat, and simmer for 50 to 60 minutes, or until the meat is tender.

Meanwhile, in a small saucepan, melt the remaining 2 tablespoons butter, and sauté the sesame seeds. Cook the noodles according to package directions, drain, and toss with the butter and sesame seeds. Keep warm in the oven.

When the veal is done, blend in the paprika and sour cream; cook just until heated. Serve at once over hot noodles. Serves 6 to 8.

VEAL STEW WITH VEGETABLES

6 tablespoons all-purpose flour
2 teaspoons salt
pepper to taste
2 pounds veal, cubed
6 tablespoons sweet butter
¾ cup peeled and chopped onion
½ pound mushrooms, peeled and sliced
¼ cup chopped parsley
2 cups Kathy's Basic Chicken Stock (page 71) or canned broth (check the label)
1 cup commercial sour cream
1½ cups peeled and sliced carrots
1 10-ounce package frozen peas, thawed and drained

On waxed paper, combine 4 tablespoons of the flour with the salt and pepper. Thoroughly coat the veal cubes with this mixture.

In a large skillet, melt the butter; brown the veal on all sides. Remove the veal from the skillet, and set aside. In the skillet, add the onion, mushrooms, and parsley; sauté, stirring, over medium heat, until the onions are golden—about 5 minutes. Remove the skillet from the heat.

Stir in the remaining 2 tablespoons flour, and blend in the stock. Return the skillet to the heat, and cook, stirring, until the sauce is thickened. Reduce the heat. Blend in the sour cream, and add the veal. Simmer, covered, for 1 hour. Add the carrots, and cook, covered, for 20 minutes. Add the peas, and cook, covered, for 5 minutes more. Serves 6.

ℋ——————

BRAISED VEAL SHANKS

4 veal shanks,
   about 3 pounds
3–4 tablespoons all-purpose
   flour
2 tablespoons pure vegetable
   oil
1 cup Kathy's Basic Chicken
   Stock (page 71) or
   canned broth (check the
   label)

2 teaspoons salt
pepper to taste
1 tablespoon lemon juice
4 carrots, peeled and halved
4 small onions, peeled
2 stalks celery, quartered
2 potatoes, peeled and
   quartered

Preheat oven to 350°. Remove the excess fat from the shanks, and wipe them with damp paper towels. Coat them well with the flour.

In a dutch oven, slowly heat the oil. Brown the shanks well on all sides. Add the chicken stock, salt, pepper, and lemon juice; cover, and bake for 1¼ to 1½ hours, or until the veal is almost tender. Turn the shanks. Add the carrots, onions, celery, and potatoes; cover, and continue to bake for an additional 35 to 45 minutes, or until the meat and vegetables are tender. Serve the meat on a platter surrounded by the vegetables. Serves 4 to 6.

ℋ——————

VEAL WAIKIKI

3 pounds veal shoulder,
   cut into 2-inch cubes
2 cups Kathy's Basic Chicken
   Stock (page 71) or
   canned broth (check the
   label)

2 8-ounce cans unsweetened
   crushed pineapple
2 onions, peeled and sliced
salt and pepper to taste
3 tablespoons all-purpose
   flour

In a large dutch oven or heavy skillet, combine the veal with all the ingredients except for the flour. Bring to a slow boil, reduce heat, and simmer, covered, until the meat is fork-tender—approximately 2½ hours. Remove 1 cup of the liquid to a bowl, and stir in the flour. Return this to the pot, and cook, stirring, until thickened. Serves 6.

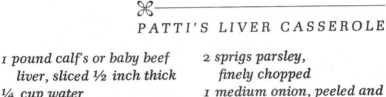

PATTI'S LIVER CASSEROLE

1 pound calf's or baby beef liver, sliced ½ inch thick
¼ cup water
3 tablespoons Cleo Jeppson's Bread Crumbs (page 262)
4 large mushrooms, finely chopped
2 sprigs parsley, finely chopped
1 medium onion, peeled and finely chopped
½ teaspoon salt
pinch of pepper

Preheat oven to 350°. Place the liver in a baking dish with the water. In a medium bowl, combine the remaining ingredients; sprinkle over the liver and bake for 45 minutes. Serves 2.

ETHEL'S THREE-IN-ONE CASSEROLE

1 tablespoon pure vegetable oil
3 green onions, chopped
1 cup cooked brown rice
1 cup Kathy's Basic Beef Stock (page 71) or canned broth (check the label)
1½ cups chopped cooked meat (any kind)
2 cups cooked whole-kernel corn
¼ cup chopped black olives
salt and pepper to taste
½ cup grated white Cheddar cheese

Preheat oven to 375°. Grease a casserole. In a skillet, heat the oil, and sauté the onions until golden brown. Add the rice, beef stock, meat, corn, olives, and salt and pepper, and stir. Pour into the casserole, and top with the grated cheese. Bake for about 20 minutes, or until heated through and the cheese is melted. Serves 6.

LEFTOVER HASH

For a recipe such as this, it may be easier to snip the parsley with kitchen shears than to chop it. Remember to use Cleo Jeppson's Bread Crumbs (page 262)—that way you can be sure that the crumbs are pure.

4 tablespoons sweet butter
½ pound pure pork sausage meat (check the label)
2 onions, peeled and chopped
4 cups ground or chopped cooked beef or poultry
salt and pepper to taste
1 cup chopped parsley
1 cup Cleo Jeppson's Bread Crumbs (page 262)

Preheat oven to 350°. Grease a casserole well.

In a skillet, heat 1 tablespoon of the butter; sauté the sausage meat and onions. Stir in the ground or chopped meat, and season with salt and pepper.

In the casserole, spread out the sausage mixture. Top with the chopped parsley and bread crumbs. Dot with the remaining 3 tablespoons butter, and bake for 1 hour. Serves 4 to 6.

❀————————————————————

FRUITS WITH MEATS

Any or all of these fruits are perfect accompaniments to ham, chicken, or curried meats or fowl.

3 bananas	*6 pineapple spears,*
1 papaya	*cut from fresh pineapple*
juice of 1 lemon	*3 tablespoons sweet butter*

Peel the bananas, and slice them in half lengthwise. Peel and slice the papaya lengthwise (keep the papaya seeds for Papaya-Seed Dressing, page 226). Squeeze the lemon juice over the prepared bananas, pineapple, and papaya, and let stand for 15 minutes. In a large skillet, melt the butter, and cook the fruit slowly, turning so that all sides brown slightly. Serves 6.

FISH AND SEAFOOD

PUFFY BROILED FISH

4 filets of sole,
about 1½ pounds
1 cup homemade
mayonnaise
(page 223)
3 tablespoons grated
Parmesan cheese
1 onion, peeled and
thinly sliced

Arrange the fish filets in a single layer in a baking dish. In a bowl, mix the mayonnaise with the cheese. Top the fish with the onion slices and mayonnaise mixture. Cover with foil, and broil for 15 minutes, removing the foil for the last few minutes in order to brown the filets. Serves 3 to 4.

FILET OF SOLE FLO

6 filets of sole,
about 2 pounds
salt and pepper to taste
2 teaspoons homemade
mustard (page 158)
1 cup homemade
mayonnaise
(page 223)

Preheat oven to 350°. In a large, shallow baking dish, arrange the fish filets in a single layer. Season with salt and pepper.

In a small bowl, mix together the mayonnaise and mustard; spread over the filets to cover. Bake for 15 to 20 minutes, or until the fish flakes when tested. Serves 4 to 6.

❈─────────────────

FISH ON SKEWERS

2 pounds haddock
¼ cup commercial sour
   cream
¼ cup lemon juice,
   freshly squeezed

2 tablespoons sweet butter,
   melted
¼ cup finely chopped parsley

─────────────────────────────

Cut the fish into 1½-inch cubes. In a small bowl, combine the sour cream and lemon juice, and mix together well. Coat the fish cubes thoroughly with the mixture. Thread the cubes close together on skewers, leaving a few inches of space at each end.

Broil, preferably over a charcoal fire, 3 to 4 inches from the heat, for about 10 minutes, or until tender. Baste occasionally with the melted butter and the remaining sour cream mixture. Turn the skewers frequently to allow the fish to brown evenly on all sides. Remove the fish cubes from the skewers, sprinkle with parsley, and serve immediately. Serves 4.

❈─────────────────

HOT OR COLD FRESH SALMON

Any whole fish can be baked wrapped in foil. The fish does not dry out, and the cooking odors do not permeate the house. If possible, buy a piece of salmon cut from the tail end, since it has fewer bones.

To serve this dish hot, present it on a platter with sour cream, boiled potatoes, and green peas. To serve it cold, chill and serve with ½ cup of homemade mayonnaise (page 223) mixed with 1 tablespoon homemade mustard (page 158).

1 tablespoon pure vegetable
oil

1 3-pound piece of salmon
aluminum foil

Preheat oven to 350°. Oil well one side of a piece of aluminum foil large enough to hold the salmon. Place the salmon on the oiled side of the foil, and wrap it up completely. Place this on a baking sheet, and bake for 45 minutes for a thinner piece, 1 hour if thicker. Serves 4 for dinner, 10 or 12 as an appetizer.

ℋ BAKED FISH WITH LEMON-BUTTER SAUCE

If the sauce separates because your stove is too hot, add an ice cube, stir slowly, and the sauce will become smooth again.

½ cup sweet butter
2 tablespoons all-purpose
flour
¼ cup lemon juice
1 cup milk

1 piece of fish, such as
haddock, halibut, or
red snapper,
½ pound per person
salt and pepper to taste

Preheat oven to 350°. In a saucepan, melt the butter; stir in the flour and lemon juice until well blended. Slowly add the milk, and cook over low heat for 5 minutes.

Season the fish with salt and pepper. Arrange the pieces in a single layer in a casserole, and pour the sauce over them. Bake for 45 minutes to 1 hour, depending on the thickness of the fish, until it flakes easily when tested with a fork. Serves 4 to 6.

BAKED HADDOCK WITH POTATOES

10 tablespoons sweet butter
4 haddock steaks,
  about 2 pounds
salt and pepper to taste
1½ pounds potatoes

1 small onion, peeled and
  thinly sliced
3 tablespoons chopped
  parsley
3 tablespoons Cleo Jeppson's
  Bread Crumbs (page 262)

Preheat oven to 400°. Grease a large metal baking dish with 3 tablespoons of the butter. Sprinkle the fish with salt and pepper, and arrange it in a single layer in the dish.

Peel and thinly slice the potatoes, plunging the slices immediately into cold water to prevent discoloring; drain well. Arrange the potato slices around and in between, but not on top of, the pieces of fish.

Lay the onion slices over the potatoes, and season the vegetables to taste. Generously dot all with the remaining 7 tablespoons butter. (Do not add any water; the fish provides its own liquid.)

Place the baking dish over the stove burner, and bring to a boil. Remove the dish to the oven, and bake, uncovered, for 15 minutes. Baste with the pan juices, and continue baking for 20 minutes, basting occasionally.

In a small bowl, combine the parsley and bread crumbs; sprinkle this over the fish and vegetables, and bake for 10 minutes longer. Serves 4 to 6.

✵————————————————

SALMON SOUFFLÉ

This soufflé can be partially prepared ahead of time and refrigerated before adding the egg whites.

4 tablespoons sweet butter	*⅛ teaspoon pepper*
1 tablespoon grated Parmesan cheese	*½ teaspoon oregano*
	4 egg yolks
2 tablespoons peeled and minced onion	*1 16-ounce can salmon, shredded*
3 tablespoons whole-wheat pastry flour	*½ cup grated white Swiss cheese*
1 cup very hot milk	*5 egg whites, beaten stiff*
½ teaspoon salt	

Preheat oven to 400°. Grease a 1½-quart soufflé or casserole dish with 1 tablespoon of the butter, and sprinkle with the Parmesan cheese.

In a saucepan, melt the remaining 3 tablespoons butter; cook the onion until soft. Add the flour, hot milk, salt, pepper, and oregano. Bring to a boil, and cook, stirring, for 1 minute. Remove from stove. Beat in the 4 egg yolks, one at a time, and add the salmon and Swiss cheese.

In a large bowl, beat the 5 egg whites until stiff; fold into the salmon mixture. Gently pour the mixture into the soufflé or casserole dish. Place the dish in the oven, and immediately reduce heat to 375°—do not open the oven door. Bake for 30 minutes, or until golden brown. Serves 6.

✂———————

SHRIMP SCAMPI

For a more festive look, lemon slices may be added with the parsley as a garnish.

½ cup pure olive oil
½ cup sweet butter
2 pounds raw shrimp
　　washed, peeled, and
　　deveined
1 tablespoon lemon juice

¼ cup peeled and chopped
　　shallots or green onions
1 teaspoon salt
pepper to taste
¼ cup finely chopped
　　parsley

———————

In a large skillet, heat the oil and butter. When the oil is very hot, add all the remaining ingredients except for the parsley; cook for a few minutes over medium heat, stirring constantly, just until the shrimp turn color—do not overcook, or the shrimp will be rubbery. Garnish with parsley. Serves 8.

✂———————

SHRIMP WITH DILL

2 pounds raw shrimp,
　　peeled and deveined
1 cup plain, additive-free
　　yogurt
salt and pepper to taste
1 teaspoon caraway seeds

4 tablespoons pure vegetable
　　oil
¾ cup finely chopped
　　fresh dillweed
　　　　or
¼ cup dried dillweed

———————

Clean the shrimp; dry, and set aside. In a medium bowl, combine the yogurt, salt and pepper, and caraway seeds.

Add the shrimp, and mix together well. Cover, and refrigerate until ready to use.

In a deep skillet or casserole, heat the oil. Add the shrimp mixture, stirring gently. Cover, and cook for a few minutes until the shrimp change color. Sprinkle with the dillweed, and serve at once (the pan juices will be quite liquid). Serves 6 to 8.

SCALLOPS À LA MARÉCHALE

Serve these tender scallops on toast for a delicious appetizer.

1 pound scallops
2 tablespoons sweet butter
1 teaspoon all-purpose flour
½ cup Kathy's Basic Chicken Stock (page 71) or canned broth (check the label)

1 teaspoon dry mustard
1 tablespoon grated Parmesan cheese
1 tablespoon minced green onion
1 tablespoon finely chopped parsley

Wash the scallops well, and cut them into quarters. In a medium saucepan, melt the butter. Add the scallops, and cook for 3 or 4 minutes over medium heat (do not overcook —scallops will toughen). Remove the scallops with a slotted spoon.

To the same saucepan add the remaining ingredients, stirring until smooth. Put the scallops back in the pan, and reheat quickly. Serves 4.

꘏————————————————

OYSTER FRITTERS

2 cups all-purpose flour
1 tablespoon baking powder
1½ teaspoons salt
2 eggs, beaten
1 cup milk

1 tablespoon sweet butter,
  melted
2 cups shelled oysters,
  drained and chopped
2 cups pure vegetable oil

In a large bowl, sift together the flour, baking powder, and salt. In a separate bowl, mix together the eggs, milk, and butter. Combine the two mixtures, stirring until smooth. Stir in the oysters.

In a deep-fat fryer, heat the oil to 350°. Drop the oyster mixture by spoonfuls into the oil, and fry for about 3 minutes, or until golden brown. Drain on paper towels. Serves 4 to 6.

꘏————————————————

TUNA-MACARONI BAKE

2 tablespoons sweet butter
1 small onion, peeled and
  finely chopped
1 tablespoon all-purpose
  flour
¼ cup milk
2 7-ounce cans tuna, drained

2 cups cooked macaroni,
  boiled until barely tender
  (check the label)
2 stalks celery,
  finely chopped
¼ cup pure crushed
  potato chips

Preheat oven to 350°. Grease a casserole. In a saucepan, melt 1 tablespoon of the butter; sauté the onion, and set aside. In a separate saucepan, melt the remaining 1 tablespoon butter; stir in the flour until blended, and gradually add the milk, stirring until the sauce is thickened.

Combine all the ingredients together except for the potato chips. Mix thoroughly, and pour into the casserole. Sprinkle with the crushed potato chips. Bake for 30 minutes. Serves 4 to 6.

HOT TUNA SANDWICHES

These are delicious served on warm, homemade No-Knead Refrigerator Rolls (page 250), in pita bread, or open-faced on toast.

1 12-ounce can tuna, drained
1 cup homemade mayonnaise (page 223)
4 hard-boiled eggs, chopped
½ cup black chopped olives
½ cup grated white cheese, any kind

Preheat oven to 350°. In a bowl, mix together all of the ingredients. Pour the mixture into a casserole, cover, and bake for 10 minutes. Serve warm, as a sandwich filling. Serves 4.

GEFÜLTE FISH

This is a modern version of the old-fashioned filled fish, which traditionally called for three kinds of fish, all of different textures. This recipe uses only white fish, any kind that is available fresh from your local market. If your fish market does not grind the fish, you can grind the filet yourself in your grinder or food processor, or chop it by hand.

FISH STOCK

1 pound fish bones,
if available, from your
fish market
(optional)
1 large onion, peeled and
sliced
1 stalk celery, chopped

1 carrot, peeled and
thinly sliced
1 tablespoon chopped
parsley
1 teaspoon salt
2 quarts water

FISH BALLS

1 pound ground white fish
½ carrot, peeled and
finely grated
1 small onion, peeled and
finely grated

¼ cup matzo meal
½ teaspoon salt
¼ teaspoon pepper
2 eggs
¼ cup water

In a large pot, combine all of the fish stock ingredients. Bring to a boil, reduce heat, and simmer for 30 minutes.

Meanwhile, combine the ground fish and vegetables. Add the matzo meal, salt, and pepper, and mix together well. Add the eggs, one at a time, and beat until fluffy. Beat in the water.

Wet your hands with cold water, and form 10 balls the size of golf balls. Drop these into the simmering stock, and let simmer slowly for 45 minutes. With a slotted spoon, remove the balls from the stock.

Fish balls may be served either hot with boiled potatoes or cold with horseradish on the side. If serving cold, let the stock boil down until 1 cup remains. Pour ½ cup of the stock over 1 tablespoon unflavored gelatin. When dissolved, stir this mixture into the remaining stock. Let cool. Arrange the fish balls on a platter, and pour the stock over them. Garnish with cooked carrot slices. Refrigerate for several hours before serving, or until the gelatin has set. Serves 10.

SAUCES AND CONDIMENTS

WHITE SAUCE MIX MINNETONKA

Prepare this sauce mix in advance, and refrigerate it so that it will be handy when a quick sauce is needed. It will make six cups of white sauce. Instructions for cooking the sauce follow below.

*1⅓ cups nonfat dry milk
   powder*
¾ cup all-purpose flour

1 teaspoon salt
*½ cup sweet butter,
   softened*

In a medium bowl, stir together the dry milk powder, flour, and salt. With a pastry blender or by hand, cut in or mix the softened butter until the mixture resembles small peas. Refrigerate immediately in a tightly covered container. Keeps for at least 3 weeks.

To prepare the sauce from the mix, see the recipe that follows.

WHITE SAUCE MINNETONKA

*½ cup White Sauce Mix
Minnetonka (above)*

1 cup cold water (see Note)

In a saucepan, over medium, not high, heat, combine the mix and water. Cook, stirring constantly, until the mixture is thickened and bubbly—about 6–7 minutes.

Note: For a thinner sauce, use 1¼ cups cold water. Yields 1 cup.

❦————————————————————————

WHITE SAUCE FOR HEAVENLY CHICKEN

2 tablespoons sweet butter
2 tablespoons all-purpose
  flour

1 cup milk
salt and pepper to taste

In a medium saucepan, melt the butter; stir in the flour until well blended. Remove from the heat, and slowly add the milk, stirring constantly. Return to low heat, and cook, stirring, until the sauce is thick and creamy. Season with salt and pepper. Makes 1 cup.

❦————————————————————————

JOAN'S BLENDER HOLLANDAISE

This is a goof-proof copy of hollandaise sauce. Make it at the last minute, or reheat it in a double boiler.

3 egg yolks
dash of cayenne
1 tablespoon lemon juice

½ cup sweet butter,
  melted and hot

In a blender container, combine the egg yolks, cayenne, and lemon juice. Cover; turn the motor on and off. Remove the cover, and turn the motor to high speed. Gradually add the melted butter in a slow, steady stream. Serve warm. Makes 1 cup.

✂————————————————

MOCK SOUR CREAM

¼ cup water

1 tablespoon lemon juice

1 cup cottage cheese

¼ teaspoon salt

Place all the ingredients in a blender container. Cover and blend on high speed until smooth. Use in same way you would sour cream. Makes about 1 cup.

✂————————————————

REMOULADE SAUCE

This sauce is excellent served on sandwiches or with fish dishes.

1 cup homemade
   mayonnaise
   (page 223)

1 teaspoon chopped parsley

1 tablespoon capers, chopped
   and drained very well

½ tablespoon homemade
   mustard (page 158)

In a small bowl, combine all the ingredients. Store in a tightly covered container. Yields 1 cup.

❀————————————————

LYNN'S PINEAPPLE SAUCE

Make this sauce to pour over pork or chicken while it roasts, or use it as a basting sauce on the grill—either way it is delicious.

4 ounces Seven-Up
1 cup unsweetened
*   pineapple juice*
¼ cup pure maple syrup

juice of ½ lemon or lime
½ teaspoon garlic powder
½ teaspoon soy sauce
*   (check the label)*

———————————————————

In a bowl, combine all the ingredients; blend or stir until well mixed. Yields 1¾ cups.

❀————————————————

COCONUT MILK

Chinese or Oriental dishes often call for coconut milk. Use it as a sauce for chicken, adding it to the pan juices to make a delicious gravy. It has a delicate flavor that enhances chicken or Cornish hens.

1½ cups milk

1½ cups grated fresh or
*   unsweetened dried*
*   coconut*

———————————————————

In a medium saucepan, bring the milk just to boiling. Place the coconut in a medium bowl, and pour the hot milk over it; let stand for 20 minutes.

Strain through a sieve, pressing the coconut with a spoon to release as much milk as possible. Yields 1½ cups.

❃————————————————————

SWEET AND SOUR SAUCE

1 tablespoon cornstarch
½ cup brown sugar
6 tablespoons unsweetened
  pineapple juice

⅓ cup white distilled vinegar
2 teaspoons soy sauce
  (check the label)

In a medium saucepan, combine the cornstarch and brown sugar; add the pineapple juice, vinegar, and soy sauce, stirring to mix. Bring the mixture to a boil, then simmer, stirring constantly, for 2 minutes, or until thickened. Serve with Chicken Wings Paula (page 91). Yields ¾ cup.

❃————————————————

MILD CURRY SAUCE

Use this sauce with cooked leftover lamb, chicken, or turkey, accompanied by the Fruits with Meats on page 133. Since curry powder is of different strengths, more can be added if needed.

¼ cup pure vegetable oil
1 onion, peeled and minced
5 tablespoons all-purpose
  flour
1 cup commercial or
  homemade coconut milk
  (page 152)

1 cup milk
1 teaspoon salt
1 teaspoon ground ginger
1 teaspoon curry powder
3 tablespoons soy sauce
  (check the label)

In small pan or skillet, heat the oil. Add the onions, cover, and cook over medium heat for 10 minutes, stirring occasionally. Add the flour, and stir until smooth. Add the remaining ingredients, stirring constantly until the mixture thickens and boils. Reduce heat to very low, cover, and cook for 15 minutes. Makes 2¼ cups.

MUSTARD SAUCE FOR VEGETABLES

A great sauce to tempt non-vegetable eaters.

½ teaspoon dry mustard
½ teaspoon all-purpose flour
¼ teaspoon salt
2 egg yolks, beaten
¾ cup milk, heated
2 tablespoons white distilled vinegar

In the top of a double boiler, over hot but not boiling water, mix the mustard, flour, and salt. Add the beaten egg yolks, and mix together well with a wire whisk or fork. Slowly add the hot milk, and cook, stirring constantly, until thickened. Slowly add the vinegar, stirring constantly to mix well. Serve warm over green beans, cauliflower, or other vegetables. Yields ¾ cup.

CREAMY HORSERADISH SAUCE

Serve this with roast beef for special occasions.

¼ teaspoon salt
1 teaspoon homemade mustard (page 158)
½ cup whipping cream, beaten stiff
1 tablespoon lemon juice
3 tablespoons prepared horseradish

In a small bowl, gradually fold the salt and mustard into the whipped cream until just mixed. Fold in the lemon juice and horseradish. Makes ½ cup.

For Sour-Cream Horseradish: Substitute ½ cup commercial sour cream for the whipped cream. Serve as a dip with cocktail-size gefülte fish balls or over cold sliced beef.

�֍————————————————————————

DONNA'S ALL-PURPOSE BARBECUE SAUCE

For chicken, hamburgers, veal, lamb, or pork chops. You won't miss tomatoes if you use this sauce.

½ cup pure vegetable oil	*2 teaspoons salt*
½ cup lemon juice	*¼ teaspoon pepper*
1 tablespoon sugar	*1 teaspoon paprika*
1 tablespoon peeled and minced onion	*¼ cup water*

In a small bowl or shaker, combine all the ingredients, and mix together well. Makes 1¼ cups.

❍────────────────────────────

OLD SMOKEY MOPPING SAUCE
FOR BARBECUE

Use this on spareribs or chicken barbecued in the oven or on an outside grill.

juice of 1 lemon
2 teaspoons all-purpose
*   flour*
1 teaspoon black pepper
2 teaspoons homemade
*   mustard (page 158)*

1 clove garlic, peeled and
*   crushed*
½ teaspoon sugar
½ teaspoon salt
white distilled vinegar
1 cup sweet butter, melted

Put the first seven ingredients in a measuring cup, and fill to the 1-cup line with vinegar. Blend together well.

In a medium saucepan, melt the butter. Add the vinegar mixture, and cook over medium heat, stirring constantly, until thickened—about 3 minutes. Yields 1 cup.

❍────────────────────────────

PICKLED PINEAPPLE ELAINE

Serve on hamburgers or tuna sandwiches. The pineapple will keep for 2 weeks.

1 8-ounce can unsweetened
*   crushed pineapple,*
*   including liquid*
⅓ cup sugar

⅓ cup white distilled
*   vinegar*
½ stick cinnamon

Place all the ingredients in a medium saucepan, and bring to a boil, stirring until the sugar is dissolved. Pour the mixture into a well-washed storage jar, cover, and chill. Makes 1¼ cups.

❦————————————————————————

INSTANT PICKLED MUSTARD BEANS

Here is one of the best of the vegetable pickles.

1 cup sugar
½ cup white distilled vinegar
3 tablespoons homemade mustard (page 158)
¼ teaspoon salt

½ teaspoon instant minced onion or 1 teaspoon peeled and minced fresh onion
2 9-ounce packages frozen wax beans, thawed

————————————————————————

In a large saucepan, combine all the ingredients except for the beans. Bring to a boil, stirring until the sugar is dissolved. Add the beans, and simmer, uncovered, for 5 minutes. Remove from the heat, and let cool.

Pour the mixture into well-washed jars, cover, and refrigerate. Drain before serving, reserving the liquids to preserve the leftovers. Keeps well for several weeks in the refrigerator. Makes 4 cups.

❦————————————————————————

ELAINE'S TOMATOLESS CATSUP

½ cup white distilled vinegar
¼ cup sugar
½ teaspoon salt
1 16-ounce can sliced or diced beets, including liquid

¼ teaspoon ground cinnamon
2 tablespoons instant minced onion or peeled and grated fresh onion
⅛ teaspoon ground ginger
dash of nutmeg

————————————————————————

In a small saucepan, over medium heat, combine the vinegar, sugar, and salt. Cook, stirring, just until the sugar is dissolved; remove from heat, and let cool.

Pour this mixture into a blender container and add the remaining ingredients. (If dried onions are used, let stand for 10 minutes.) Blend until smooth. Pour into a jar with a tightly fitting lid, and refrigerate. Makes 2½ cups.

⌘ HOT MUSTARD

⅓ cup dry mustard
(see Note)
1 teaspoon salt
½ teaspoon white pepper
1 teaspoon sugar

1 tablespoon water
1 tablespoon white distilled
vinegar
1 tablespoon pure vegetable
oil

In a medium bowl, mix together the mustard, salt, pepper, and sugar. Gradually stir the liquids into the dry ingredients, pouring in a thin, steady stream and stirring constantly to keep the mixture smooth. Cover, and let stand at room temperature for at least 1 hour before serving. Store, covered, in the refrigerator. Makes ½ cup.

Note: For a really hot English-type mustard, use ½ cup dry mustard.

⌘ SWEET AND SPICY MUSTARD

This is really quite easy to make and has a refreshingly zesty taste.

5 tablespoons dry mustard
¼ cup sugar
1 tablespoon all-purpose flour
½ teaspoon salt

2 eggs, beaten
½ cup white distilled
  vinegar
1 tablespoon sweet butter

In the top of a double boiler, combine the mustard, sugar, flour, and salt; stir to mix well. With a wire whisk or fork, beat in the eggs and then the vinegar until smooth.

Place over boiling water, and cook, stirring constantly, until thickened. Add the butter, and stir until melted. Cool the mixture; pour into a jar with a tightly fitting lid, and refrigerate. Makes 1½ cups.

SEASONED SALT

This seasoned salt is excellent for rubbing on a roast of any kind before cooking. Use it on Susie's Roast Beef Supreme (page 103) or on meats to be barbecued.

6 tablespoons salt
2½ teaspoons paprika
1 teaspoon dry mustard
½ teaspoon thyme
½ teaspoon marjoram

½ teaspoon garlic salt
½ teaspoon curry powder
½ teaspoon celery salt
¼ teaspoon onion salt
⅛ teaspoon dillseed

In a small bowl, mix together all the ingredients. Store in a covered jar. Makes about ½ cup.

VEGETABLES

BEST BAKED BEANS

This recipe from Minnesota is great for a potluck supper. Rather than white beans, you can use canned green lima beans or any combination that adds interest and taste.

*1 pound sliced bacon
 (check the label)*
1 onion, peeled and chopped
*2 15-ounce cans red kidney
 beans, drained*
¼ cup brown sugar

*2 15-ounce cans butter
 beans, drained*
*2 15-ounce cans pork and
 beans (check the label)*
½ teaspoon dry mustard
dash of pepper

Preheat oven to 350°. In a skillet, fry the bacon; drain on paper towels, and break the bacon into small pieces. In the remaining bacon fat, sauté the onion.

In a large bowl, mix together the remaining ingredients. Add the bacon and onion, and put into a casserole. Bake for 1 hour. Serves 10 to 12.

OLD-FASHIONED BAKED BEANS

*1 pound dried small white
 beans*
1½ teaspoons salt
1 teaspoon dry mustard
1½ teaspoons black pepper
dash of cayenne
*½ cup peeled and
 chopped onion*

*¼ cup unsulphured
 molasses or honey*
¼ cup brown sugar
*¼ cup white distilled
 vinegar*
1 quart boiling water
*¼ pound cubed bacon
 (check the label)*

Soak the beans overnight in water; drain. Preheat oven to 300°. Add the salt, mustard, pepper, and cayenne to the beans, and mix together well. Stir in the onion, molasses or honey, brown sugar, and vinegar. Pour half the mixture into a 2-quart baking dish. Add half the bacon, then the rest of the beans. Top with the remaining bacon. Pour in the water to the top of beans. Cover. Bake for 6 hours. (Additional water may be needed as the beans cook down.) Serves 6.

ANGELA'S BROCCOLI

This Italian-style broccoli may be served either hot or cold— a nutritious dish either way, since broccoli is high in vitamin C.

1½ pounds fresh broccoli
6 teaspoons pure olive oil,
    or more to taste

juice of 1 lemon
salt and pepper to taste

In a saucepan, steam or boil the broccoli until just tender, not soft. Cut off part of the stems, reserving them for soup if you wish. Pour the olive oil and lemon juice over the broccoli heads, season, and serve at once. Serves 6.

✂ ———————————————————
DELICIOUS CABBAGE

3 tablespoons pure vegetable
   oil
1 cup peeled and
   chopped onion
1 3-pound head cabbage,
   cored and shredded
1 teaspoon caraway seeds

¼ cup white distilled
   vinegar
1 cup water
½ teaspoon salt
1 tablespoon honey
pepper to taste

In a large saucepan, heat the oil, and sauté the onion until it is transparent. Stir in the cabbage, and mix to coat with the oil and onions. Add the caraway seeds. Cover the pan, and steam over low heat for 10 minutes. Pour in the vinegar and water, and stir to blend. Add the salt, honey, and pepper. Cover, and cook over low heat for 10 minutes. Serve immediately. Serves 4.

✂ ———————————————————
CARROT RING

Fill the center of this attractive ring with buttered peas or beans, creamed tuna, crab, or asparagus.

2 cups puréed peeled and
   cooked carrots
1 teaspoon peeled and
   minced onion
3 eggs, well beaten

1 cup milk
2 tablespoons sweet butter,
   melted
1 teaspoon salt
pepper to taste

Preheat oven to 350°. Generously grease a ring mold. In a large bowl, mix all ingredients in the order listed, one at a time, stirring well after each addition. Pour the mixture into the ring mold. Set the mold on a folded cloth in a shallow pan; fill the pan 1 inch deep with hot water. Bake for 40 minutes. Remove the ring mold from the oven, and let stand for a few minutes. Loosen the edges, and invert the carrot ring onto a large, hot platter. Serves 6.

HONEY-GLAZED CARROTS

Make these carrots while preparing a chicken dish so that you will have chicken fat on hand.

12 small or 6 large carrots
1½ tablespoons chicken fat
   or sweet butter

¼ cup honey

Peel the carrots, and quarter them if large. In a saucepan, cook the carrots in boiling salted water until tender. Drain thoroughly, and allow to stand for a few minutes to dry.

In a skillet, heat the fat or butter and honey, and stir until blended. Add the carrots. Simmer slowly, turning frequently, until browned and glazed. Serves 4.

GINGERED CARROTS

You can keep fresh ginger in the freezer, and it will be handy when needed. A little goes a long way.

4 medium carrots
½ cup water
1 teaspoon sugar or
   1 tablespoon ginger
  marmalade
  (check the label)

1 teaspoon peeled and
  grated ginger
2 tablespoons sweet butter
chopped parsley for garnish

Peel the carrots, and cut them into strips. In a sauce pan, simmer the carrot strips in the water over low heat for about 10 minutes, or until tender but firm. Add the sugar or marmalade, ginger, and butter. Cook for 2 or 3 minutes longer, turning the carrots carefully several times to coat them and to reduce the liquid. Serve hot, garnished with parsley. Serves 4.

✿ JANE'S CELERY PARMESAN

1 large bunch celery
1 cup commercial sour cream
salt and pepper to taste

½ cup grated Parmesan
  cheese
1 tablespoon sweet butter

Preheat oven to 350°. Wash the celery well, and trim, cutting off the strings. Cut the celery into 1-inch pieces, and place them in a saucepan with just enough water to cover. Boil until tender—25 to 30 minutes. Drain well in a colander, reserving the liquid for soup if you wish.

Place the celery in a baking dish. Pour the sour cream on top, and season with salt and pepper. Cover with Parmesan cheese, and dot with butter. Bake until hot—15 to 20 minutes. Serves 6.

❏─────────────

CORN PUDDING

12 ears corn
2 eggs, separated
1 tablespoon sweet butter
   melted
½ cup milk

¼ teaspoon baking powder
½ teaspoon salt
2 tablespoons all-purpose
   flour

Preheat oven to 325°. Grease a baking dish. Grate the raw corn from the cobs. (If the corn is very fresh, it will spatter, so be sure to wear an apron and grate into a bowl over the sink.)

In a large bowl, beat the egg yolks. Beat in the butter and milk. Add the corn and the remaining dry ingredients, mixing thoroughly. In a separate bowl, beat the egg whites until stiff. Fold the egg whites into the corn mixture. Pour into the baking dish, and bake for 1 hour. Serves 6.

❏─────────────

ITALIAN EGGPLANT PATTIES

1 medium eggplant,
   peeled and cubed
1¼ cups matzo meal
1¼ cups grated white
   Cheddar cheese
2 eggs, slightly beaten
2 tablespoons chopped
   parsley

2 tablespoons chopped green
   onions
1 clove garlic, peeled and
   minced
½ teaspoon salt
pinch of pepper
4 tablespoons pure olive oil

In a covered saucepan, boil the eggplant cubes in salted water until tender—about 5 minutes. Drain well. In a large bowl, mash the eggplant; stir in all the remaining ingredients except for the olive oil. Shape into patties about 3 inches in diameter.

In a skillet, heat the oil. Fry the patties until golden brown and cooked through; turn, and brown other side—about 3 to 5 minutes on each side. Serves 4 to 6.

⌘————————————

EGGPLANT SLICES

½ large eggplant,
  cut lengthwise
¼ pound white Wisconsin
  brick cheese
1 egg, beaten

2 sprigs parsley, chopped
salt to taste
¼ cup pure vegetable oil or
  sweet butter

Place the eggplant, skin side up, on a carving board. With a sharp knife, cut off and discard the ends. Cut the first slice about ⅛ inch thick, but not all the way through. Cut the next slice the same width, but cut through to the board—that is, each ¼-inch slice will contain a pocket. Continue in this manner until the entire eggplant has been sliced.

In a bowl, grate the cheese. Add half the egg, the parsley, and the salt. Fill each eggplant pocket with a small amount of this mixture, and close with uncolored toothpicks. Dip the eggplant slices in the remaining egg to coat each full slice.

In a skillet, slowly heat the oil. Fry the eggplant slices over medium heat until tender. Serves 4 to 6.

✂ ────────────────────

STUFFED EGGPLANT

For a tasty variation, substitute ¼ pound pure ground pork sausage or lamb in place of the clams, frying the meat a little longer.

8 tablespoons sweet butter
1 large eggplant
2 small onions, peeled and
    sliced
1 tablespoon chopped
    parsley

1 6-ounce can minced clams,
    drained (reserve juice)
1 egg yolk, beaten
1 cup Cleo Jeppson's Bread
    Crumbs (page 262)
salt and pepper to taste

In a large skillet, slowly heat 4 tablespoons of the butter. Cut the eggplant in half lengthwise. Fry it, cut side down, until soft (the skin will change color). Cool, and scoop out the pulp, preserving the shell.

Preheat oven to 325°. In the same skillet, melt the remaining 4 tablespoons butter. Sauté the onions, parsley, and eggplant pulp until soft. Stir in the clams, half the clam juice, the egg yolk, half the bread crumbs, and the salt and pepper. Cook until heated through.

Stuff the mixture back into the eggplant shells, and top with the remaining ½ cup bread crumbs. Bake until browned—about 20 to 25 minutes. Serves 2 generously.

✿———————————————
BERNICE'S MUSHROOM MUFFINS

3 tablespoons sweet butter
½ pound mushrooms,
   finely chopped
2 cups all-purpose flour
1 tablespoon baking powder
½ teaspoon salt

2 teaspoons sugar
1 cup grated white Cheddar
   cheese
2 eggs, beaten
¾ cup milk

Preheat oven to 375°. Generously grease 12 muffin cups. In a skillet, melt the butter, and sauté mushrooms until golden. Remove from heat.

In a large bowl, sift together the dry ingredients, and stir in the cheese. In a separate bowl, stir together the eggs, milk, and mushrooms. Add these to the dry ingredients, and mix just until blended. Spoon the mixture into the muffin tins. Bake for 30 minutes, or until lightly browned. Makes 12 muffins.

✿———————————————
CREAMED MUSHROOMS

1½ pounds fresh
   mushrooms, quartered
5 tablespoons sweet butter

3 tablespoons all-purpose
   flour
1 cup milk
salt and pepper to taste

Sauté the mushrooms in 2 tablespoons of the butter; do not brown. In a saucepan, melt the remaining 3 tablespoons butter over medium heat. Stir in the flour. Slowly add the milk, beating with a wire whisk until the mixture starts to boil and get very thick. Season with salt and pepper. Stir in the mushrooms, and heat through. Serves 6 generously.

�֍————————————————————————————

MUSHROOMS IN SOUR CREAM SAUCE

This sauce is equally good for meats or vegetables, and it is great served with the Spinach-Noodle Ring (page 178).

2 tablespoons sweet butter
2 small onions, peeled and
  finely chopped
½ cup commercial sour
  cream

salt and white pepper to taste
½ pound mushrooms,
  sautéed

————————————————————————————

In a skillet, melt the butter, and sauté the onions until they are transparent. In a bowl, combine the sour cream and onions, and season with salt and pepper. Heat briefly, and stir in the mushrooms. Yields ½ cup.

�֍————————————————————————————

COLIN AND ROBYN'S ONION QUICHE

This delicious quiche was a treat at buffets in Adelaide, Australia.

½ recipe Elaine's Piecrust
  (page 297)
2 tablespoons sweet butter
1 pound onions, peeled and
  finely diced
1 or 2 rashers finely chopped
  bacon (check the label)
3 eggs

1 cup less 1 tablespoon
  light cream
salt and pepper to taste
¼ teaspoon nutmeg
½ teaspoon dry mustard
¾ cup finely grated white
  Cheddar cheese

————————————————————————————

Preheat oven to 350°. Fit the piecrust into a quiche pan or large pie plate. In a skillet, melt the butter; cook the onions gently until soft but not browned. Remove from heat, and let cool. Cook the bacon in the same pan.

In a medium bowl, beat together the eggs and cream until blended, and beat in the salt and pepper, the nutmeg, and the mustard. Place the onions on the bottom of piecrust, and sprinkle with the cheese. Carefully pour the egg mixture over this, and top with the finely chopped bacon. Bake for 35 to 45 minutes, or until set and lightly browned. Cool for 10 minutes before serving. Serve either warm or cold. Serves 6 to 8.

✼ MASHED POTATOES

Since a number of our recipes call for mashed potatoes, we have included this basic recipe. The package mixes are taboo because of their preservatives.

6 *medium potatoes*	*⅓ cup hot milk*
3 *tablespoons sweet butter*	*1 teaspoon salt*

Peel the potatoes, cover with salted water, and boil for 30 minutes. Drain the potatoes, let them cool slightly, and rub them through a sieve to mash. Add the remaining ingredients, and beat with a fork or wooden spoon until fluffy. Reheat in a double boiler. Makes 3 cups.

SCALLOPED POTATOES

6–8 medium potatoes
1½ teaspoons salt
3 tablespoons all-purpose
  flour
¼ teaspoon pepper

3 large onions, peeled and
  thinly sliced
2 cups milk, scalded
2 tablespoons sweet butter

Preheat oven to 375°. Grease a 2½-quart baking dish. Peel the potatoes, and slice them thinly. In a saucepan, cover the potatoes with water, add ½ teaspoon of the salt, and parboil. Drain.

Arrange a layer of half the potatoes in the baking dish. Sprinkle with half the flour, the remaining 1 teaspoon salt, and the pepper. Then top with half the onions. Repeat the layers.

Pour the hot milk over the potatoes, dot with the butter, cover, and bake for 45 minutes. Uncover, and bake for 15 minutes longer, or until the potatoes are tender and the top is browned. Serves 6.

FANCY MASHED POTATOES

8–10 medium potatoes,
  peeled and boiled
1 8-ounce package cream
  cheese, softened
1 cup commercial sour
  cream

¼ cup peeled and
  grated onion
1 teaspoon garlic powder
  (optional)
2 teaspoons sweet butter
dash of paprika

Preheat oven to 350°. In a large bowl, mash the potatoes; beat in the cream cheese, sour cream, onion, and garlic powder. Pour the mixture into a greased baking dish. Dot with butter, and sprinkle with paprika. Bake for 30 to 40 minutes. Serves 8.

ITALIAN POTATO RING VICKIE

2 pounds potatoes, peeled
7 tablespoons sweet butter
4 eggs, beaten
1 tablespoon chopped
    parsley
salt and pepper to taste

¼ pound mozzarella cheese,
    grated
2 tablespoons grated
    Parmesan cheese
3 tablespoons Cleo Jeppson's
    Bread Crumbs (page 262)

Preheat oven to 350°. Melt 1 tablespoon of the butter and grease a 1½-quart ring mold with it. Boil the potatoes in salted water until tender. Drain and mash. Blend in 5 tablespoons of the butter, the eggs, parsley, salt and pepper, and mozzarella cheese.

In a cup, mix the Parmesan cheese with 2 tablespoons of the bread crumbs; sprinkle this over the sides and bottom of the ring mold. Pour in the potato mixture, leveling the top with a spoon. Sprinkle with the remaining 1 tablespoon bread crumbs, dot with the remaining 1 tablespoon butter, and bake for 35 minutes. Remove from oven and let stand for a few minutes. Loosen the edges and invert the ring onto a large hot platter. Serves 6 to 8.

✂———————————————————————

EASY SKILLET POTATOES

Since these are parboiled, they are real time savers.

4 medium potatoes	1 tablespoon sweet butter
3 tablespoons pure peanut oil	salt and pepper to taste

———————————————————————

Place the unpeeled potatoes in a saucepan, and add enough cold salted water to cover. Bring the water to a boil, and simmer for 15 to 20 minutes, or just until tender—do not overcook. Let the potatoes cool enough to peel. Cut them into ¼-inch slices.

In a heavy skillet, heat the oil and butter. Add the potato slices, and season with salt and pepper. Cook over medium heat, shaking the skillet occasionally to redistribute the potatoes, until they form a crisp crust on the bottom and are nicely browned. (If you wish a crisp crust on both sides, turn the potatoes after they are browned on the bottom, and continue cooking until the second side is browned.) Serve hot. Serves 4.

✂———————————————————————

OVEN-BAKED FRENCH FRIES

A busy mother will find these excellent.

2 medium potatoes	salt to taste
1 tablespoon pure vegetable oil	

———————————————————————

Chill the potatoes; then peel them and cut them into frenchfry sticks. Preheat oven to 450°. Pour the oil into the center of a large baking sheet. Add the cut potatoes, and mix by hand until coated. Spread the potatoes out evenly over the baking sheet, and salt them. Bake for 35 to 40 minutes, or until golden brown, watching carefully and turning once. Serves 2.

GRATED POTATO PUDDING

6 large potatoes
¼ small onion, peeled and
   grated
3 eggs, well beaten
1 cup hot milk

6 tablespoons sweet butter,
   softened
2½ teaspoons salt
¼ cup chopped parsley

Preheat oven to 350°. Generously grease a shallow baking dish. Peel the potatoes, and grate them. In a large bowl, combine with the grated onion. Stir in the beaten eggs, hot milk, butter, salt, and parsley. Pour this mixture into the baking dish. Bake for 1¼ hours. Serves 8 to 10.

RICH POTATO PANCAKES

4 large potatoes
¾ cup milk
4 eggs
3 tablespoons heavy cream

3 tablespoons all-purpose
   flour
salt and pepper to taste
5 tablespoons sweet butter

Peel the potatoes, and in a large saucepan, cook them in boiling salted water until they are just tender. Drain, and dry thoroughly. Mash, putting them through a fine sieve.

In a small saucepan, heat the milk. Beat the milk into the potatoes and let the mixture cool completely. Stir in the eggs, cream, and flour, and season with salt and pepper. (The mixture should have the consistency of very thick cream; if it is too thick, add more cream.)

In a large skillet, melt the butter over medium heat. Drop the potato mixture into the skillet by teaspoonfuls, keeping space between the pancakes to allow for spread while cooking. When the pancakes are browned, turn and brown the other side. As they are finished, pile them on a napkin on a heated dish. Serve immediately, with Norma's Pear Sauce (page 316) or commercial sour cream. Serves 4.

✿

SPINACH-NOODLE RING

This is excellent party fare for a crowd. For a beautiful presentation, fill the center of the mold with fresh creamed or sautéed mushrooms, or mushrooms in sour cream with sautéed onions.

6 eggs, lightly beaten
4 10-ounce packages frozen
  chopped spinach,
  cooked and drained well
1 cup sweet butter
2 medium onions,
  peeled and chopped

2 8-ounce packages medium
  noodles (check the label),
  cooked, drained, and
  rinsed
1 teaspoon salt,
  or more to taste
1 cup commercial sour cream

Preheat oven to 350°. Generously grease a 3-quart ring mold.

In a large bowl, mix the eggs and cooked spinach. In a skillet, heat the butter, and sauté the onions; mix the onions into the spinach. Fold the spinach mixture into the cooked noodles, add the salt and sour cream, and mix together well. Pour the mixture into the mold.

Place the ring mold in a pan of hot water that reaches up to the rim of the mold, and bake for 45 minutes, or until set. Unmold. Serves 20 to 24.

✿ ALAN'S SPINACH CASSEROLE

Many more men are enjoying cooking these days, and many prove to be excellent cooks, as this recipe illustrates.

1 10-ounce package frozen chopped spinach
¾ cup milk
1 tablespoon sweet butter
2 eggs, lightly beaten
¾ cup grated white Swiss cheese

½ teaspoon salt
dash of pepper
1 teaspoon instant minced onion
1 2-ounce can mushrooms, drained
dash of nutmeg

Preheat oven to 325°. Grease a casserole. In a saucepan, cook the spinach according to package directions. Drain. In a separate saucepan, heat the milk and butter. Remove from the heat, and add the eggs, Swiss cheese, salt, pepper, onion, mushrooms, and spinach. Mix together well. Place the mixture in the casserole, and sprinkle with nutmeg. Bake for 50 to 60 minutes, or until set. Serves 4.

❀————————————————————

SPINACH AND COTTAGE CHEESE
FOR FIFTY

This recipe is included for the Feingold associations, since many have affairs where large amounts are needed. It is simple, inexpensive, and can be served cold.

15 pounds spinach	*3 pounds walnuts, chopped*
7 pounds cottage cheese	*2 ounces nutmeg*

Wash and drain the spinach thoroughly, then boil or steam it until cooked; drain. Mix the spinach with the cottage cheese, walnuts, and nutmeg. Serve either hot or cold. Serves 50.

❀————————————————————

COCONUT-MILK SPINACH

2 10-ounce packages frozen spinach	*½ teaspoon prepared horseradish*
1 cup commercial or homemade coconut milk (page 152)	*1 teaspoon salt*

Cook the spinach according to package directions. Drain, and place it in a blender container with half the coconut milk; purée. Add the horseradish, salt, and the remaining coconut milk. In a double boiler over hot but not boiling water, cook the mixture until heated through. Serves 4.

✂ SPINACH FRITTATA

2 10-ounce packages frozen
　chopped spinach, thawed
4 eggs
½ cup matzo meal
½ cup milk
½ cup crumbled feta cheese

½ cup grated Parmesan
　cheese
¼ cup crumbled farmer
　cheese
¼ teaspoon salt
pinch of pepper

Preheat oven to 375°. Grease a baking dish. Drain the spinach thoroughly. In a large bowl, combine with all the remaining ingredients except for ¼ cup of the Parmesan cheese. Spoon the mixture into the baking dish. Sprinkle with the reserved cheese. Bake for 40 minutes, or until the top is browned. Serves 6 to 8.

✂ SPAGHETTI SQUASH JASON

This is a vegetable that was introduced here from the Orient a few years ago. It can be found at vegetable stands and in many food markets. If you see it, get it—you will be in for a real treat. The strands come apart like spaghetti—hence, the name. It can be served with Basic Spaghetti Sauce (page 201), for a big surprise.

1 spaghetti squash
2 tablespoons sweet butter,
　melted

4 tablespoons grated
　Parmesan cheese

Preheat oven to 350°. Place the whole squash on a baking sheet, and bake for 55 minutes. Remove from the oven. Quarter the squash, and remove the seeds. Brush with the melted butter, and sprinkle with the Parmesan cheese. Serves 4.

✿──────── BAKED YELLOW SQUASH BOATS

For both corn and squash lovers, this is a great dish. Stuffed squash boats may be frozen and baked when thawed.

4 large yellow crooked-neck squash	*1 teaspoon tarragon, crumbled*
2 ears corn or 1 8-ounce can corn kernels, drained	*1 teaspoon salt*
	pepper to taste
2 tablespoons sweet butter, melted	*½ cup water*
	1 cup soft bread crumbs (2 slices)
1 medium onion, peeled and chopped	*1 egg, beaten*

Trim the ends from the squash, and cut in half lengthwise. In a large skillet, cook the squash in boiling salted water for 10 minutes, or until just tender. Drain on paper towels, and set aside.

Meanwhile, cut the kernels from the corn. In the same skillet, melt 1 tablespoon of the butter, and sauté the onion until soft. Stir in the corn, tarragon, salt, pepper, and the water. Cover the skillet, and simmer for 10 minutes, or until the corn is tender. Stir in the bread crumbs and egg. Correct the seasoning.

Preheat oven to 350°. Scoop out the seeds from the squash halves; arrange the squash shells in a baking dish. Fill with the corn mixture, and brush the exposed cut surfaces of squash with melted butter. Bake for 15 minutes, or until the stuffing is golden brown. Serves 8.

SQUASH-RICE CASSEROLE

3 pounds squash of one or more varieties, sliced
1½ cups cooked rice
1 teaspoon salt
½ teaspoon pepper
½ teaspoon oregano
1½ cups grated white Monterey Jack cheese

⅓ cup grated Parmesan cheese
2 tablespoons sweet butter, melted
½ cup chopped pecans (optional)

Preheat oven to 350°. Boil the squash in salted water for 4 to 5 minutes; drain. Arrange the squash in a greased casserole or baking dish, and layer the rice over it. Sprinkle with the salt, pepper, and oregano, and the Jack cheese. Top with Parmesan.

In a small bowl, mix together the butter and pecans, and pour over the top of the casserole. Bake, uncovered, for 15 minutes. Serves 10.

SWEET POTATO BALLS

2½ cups cooked sweet potatoes, peeled and mashed
½ teaspoon salt
pepper to taste

2 tablespoons sweet butter, melted
⅓ cup honey
1 cup chopped walnuts

Preheat oven to 375°. In a bowl, combine the sweet potatoes, salt, pepper, and butter. Chill for 30 minutes for easier handling. Using about ¼ cup of the mixture for each ball, shape into 2-inch balls.

In a skillet, heat the honey slowly and carefully so that it doesn't burn. When hot, add the balls, one at a time, turning carefully to coat evenly. Remove them from the skillet. With two forks, roll the balls in the walnuts to coat. Place in a greased baking dish, and bake for 15 minutes. Serves 4.

⌘

TANYA'S SWEET POTATO TZIMMES

A tzimmes is traditionally made with carrots, sweet potatoes, and prunes. This one replaces the prunes with dried pears to make it acceptable for the Feingold Diet.

6 *sweet potatoes*	3 *tablespoons all-purpose*
4 *medium carrots, peeled,*	*flour*
pared, and thinly sliced	2 *cups dried pears*
3 *tablespoons sweet butter*	*salt to taste*
½ *cup sugar*	1 *teaspoon lemon juice*

Scrub the sweet potatoes well under cold water. In a large saucepan, cover with water, and bring to a boil. Reduce heat, and simmer, covered, until the sweet potatoes are half cooked—about 15 minutes. Drain, and let cool. Peel the sweet potatoes, and slice them crosswise into ½-inch-thick slices.

Preheat oven to 325°. In boiling salted water, cook the carrots until half done—about 5 to 8 minutes. Drain, reserving 1 cup of the liquid, and let cool.

In a medium saucepan, melt the butter. Stir in the sugar

and flour, a tablespoon at a time, and cook, stirring constantly, until lightly browned. Gradually stir in the carrot liquid, and set aside.

Grease a casserole. Layer the sweet potatoes, overlapping them slightly, in the bottom of the casserole; layer the carrots and pears over that. Sprinkle with salt to taste and the lemon juice. Pour the sauce over all, cover, and bake for 1 hour. Serves 6 generously.

✂ SWEET POTATO AND DATE CASSEROLE

For Thanksgiving, this is a delicious variation on the traditional sweet potato dish and tastes much like the filling of pumpkin pie.

3 eggs
½ cup milk
½ teaspoon ground
cinnamon
¾ teaspoon salt
¼ cup sweet butter,
softened

¾ cup dates, pitted
5 small canned sweet
potatoes, drained
½ cup pecan halves
(optional)

Preheat oven to 350°. Grease a baking dish.

Place the eggs, milk, cinnamon, salt, and butter in a blender container; blend for 30 seconds. Add the dates, and blend for an additional 20 seconds. Add the sweet potatoes, one at a time, blending until the mixture is smooth.

Pour the mixture into the baking dish, cover with pecan halves, and bake for 30 minutes. Serves 6.

VEGETABLE CASSEROLE

6 *medium zucchini*
4 *medium yellow crooked-*
  neck squash
2 *onions, peeled*
10 *mushrooms*
4 *carrots, peeled*
8–10 *teaspoons pure olive oil*

salt and pepper to taste
½ *cup grated white Swiss*
  cheese
1 *cup grated Parmesan*
  cheese
1 *tablespoon chopped*
  parsley

Preheat oven to 350°. Slice all the vegetables as thinly as possible. In a heavy skillet, heat the oil. Add the vegetables separately, a handful at a time; season with salt and pepper, and cook for a few minutes over medium heat, until tender, adding more oil if necessary.

In a large greased casserole, layer the vegetables separately; top with the cheese and parsley. Bake for 30 minutes. Just before serving, brown the top of the vegetables under the broiler. Serves 8 to 10.

✂——————————————————————

ZUCCHINI-CHEESE MUFFINS

If you enjoyed the zucchini pancakes in our first book, then you'll like these "muffins," to serve with dinner as a vegetable course. You can also make this in smaller muffin tins, using ½ teaspoon of oil per cup, for little children.

12 teaspoons pure vegetable oil

3 slices (about 4 ounces) provolone cheese, shredded

2 medium zucchini, grated

½ teaspoon salt

3 tablespoons peeled and finely grated onion

½ cup Cleo Jeppson's Bread Crumbs (page 262) or matzo meal

2 eggs

———————————————————————

Preheat oven to 375°. Grease each muffin cup with 1 teaspoon of the oil.

In a medium bowl, combine all the remaining ingredients, and stir well until completely blended. Spoon the batter evenly into the muffin cups. Bake for 20 minutes, or until golden brown. Makes 12 large muffins.

✂——————————————————————

JOAN'S ZUCCHINI SOUFFLÉ

1 pound zucchini

1 3-ounce package cream cheese, softened

2 eggs

salt and pepper to taste

2 tablespoons grated Parmesan cheese

dash of paprika

———————————————————————

Preheat oven to 350°. Grease a casserole. Wash and cut the zucchini into 1-inch slices. Steam until just tender; drain well. In a bowl, combine the zucchini and cream cheese, and beat until smooth. Quickly beat in the eggs and the salt and pepper until smooth. Pour the mixture into the casserole, and top with Parmesan cheese and paprika. Bake for 30 minutes. Serves 4 to 6.

✻————————————————————————

STUFFED ZUCCHINI BOATS

Prepare this in advance so that you need cook it for only twenty minutes before dinner.

6 zucchini

2 eggs, beaten

½ cup grated white Cheddar cheese

½ cup grated white Monterey Jack cheese

½ cup Cleo Jeppson's Bread Crumbs (page 262)

2 tablespoons chopped parsley

salt and pepper to taste

Preheat oven to 350°. Grease a baking sheet. In a large saucepan, boil the whole zucchini until tender but not soft. Drain well. Cut them in half lengthwise. Scoop out the center pulp, and reserve.

In a bowl, combine the reserved pulp with the remaining ingredients. Spoon the mixture back into the zucchini shells, and place on the baking sheet. Bake for 15 minutes, then raise the temperature to 450°, and cook for 5 minutes longer. Serves 6.

RICE, NOODLES, AND PASTA

This has been my favorite rice recipe for fifty years. Serve it with Chinese or Spanish dishes. It will stay fluffy, with each grain separate, on low heat.

1 cup uncooked white rice   *pinch of salt*
2¼ cups water

In a small pan with a tight-fitting cover, combine the rice, 2¼ cups of water, and the salt. Cover tightly, and cook over medium heat. As soon as the water boils, turn the heat to low. Cook for about 25 minutes, or until all the water has been absorbed—every kernel should be separate, flaky, and dry. This can be kept until needed if cooked a little in advance over very low heat. Serves 4 to 6.

✂—————————

CON QUESO RICE

From San Diego comes another Spanish dish. *Con queso* means "with cheese."

2 tablespoons pure vegetable
  oil
2 cloves garlic, peeled and
  minced
1 large onion, peeled and
  chopped

1½ cups raw brown rice
½ cup dry black beans or
  dry black-eyed peas
1 cup cottage cheese
3½ cups grated white Jack
  cheese

Preheat oven to 350°. Grease a shallow 3-quart casserole. Cook the rice and beans separately according to package directions. In a skillet, heat the oil; sauté the garlic and onion until slightly cooked.

In a bowl, mix rice, beans, garlic, and onion. In a separate bowl, mix the cottage cheese with 3 cups of the Jack cheese. Layer the rice mixture alternately with the cheese mixture in the casserole, ending with the rice. Bake for 25 minutes; sprinkle with the remaining ½ cup cheese, and bake for 5 minutes longer. Serves 8 to 10.

⚘————————————————————————

LINDA'S RED BEANS AND RICE

If served with a salad, this Louisiana specialty makes a great meal.

1 pound dry red kidney beans	*1 clove garlic, peeled and minced*
10 cups of water	*2 tablespoons finely chopped celery*
½ pound uncooked ham (check the label) or other meat	*2 tablespoons finely chopped parsley*
1 onion, peeled and chopped	*1 large bay leaf, salted*

Sort, rinse and drain the beans, and place them in a large cooking pot with the water. In a skillet, render the meat. Remove the meat from the fat, and add to the beans. Place the onion, garlic, celery, and parsley in the skillet, and lightly sauté in the drippings from the meat. Add the bay leaf, and stir into the beans. Cook slowly over low heat for 1¼ hours, adding more water if necessary. Remove 5 tablespoons of the beans, mash through a sieve, and stir back into the liquid to make it creamy. Cook for another 15 minutes. Serve over fluffy rice. Serves 6.

✂ CHINESE FRIED RICE

2 tablespoons pure vegetable oil
1 cup finely chopped cooked chicken
6 fresh mushrooms, finely chopped
4 cups cooked rice

1 green onion, including the top, finely diced
2 tablespoons soy sauce (check the label), or more to taste
1 egg, well beaten

In a skillet, heat the oil; add the chicken, mushrooms, rice, green onion, and soy sauce. Fry over low heat for 10 minutes, stirring often. Add the egg, and continue cooking, stirring, for 5 minutes longer. Serves 6 to 8.

✂ RICE MINETTE

2 tablespoons sweet butter
2 green onions, chopped
1 cup uncooked rice
3 cups Kathy's Basic Chicken Stock (page 71) or canned broth (check the label)

salt and pepper to taste
2 tablespoons chopped parsley

In a saucepan, melt the butter, and lightly cook the green onions. Add the rice, and stir until the rice is coated. Add the chicken stock. Bring the mixture to a boil, cover, and cook over medium heat for 18 minutes, or until all the liquid is absorbed. Season with salt and pepper, and sprinkle with parsley. Serve immediately. Serves 4 to 6.

✂ BULGUR PILAF

2 tablespoons pure vegetable oil
1 tablespoon peeled and chopped onion
1 cup uncooked bulgur

2 cups water or any pure stock
½ teaspoon salt
dash of pepper

In a skillet, heat the oil. Add the onion, and sauté until almost tender. Add the bulgur, and cook over medium heat, stirring often, until golden in color. Add the water or stock and the seasonings; cover, and bring to a boil. Reduce the heat, and simmer for 15 minutes. Serves 4.

✂ BARLEY-MUSHROOM PILAF

½ cup pure vegetable oil
2 cups fresh mushrooms, sliced
1 tablespoon chopped parsley
1 small onion, peeled and diced

2 cups uncooked barley
4 cups Kathy's Basic Chicken Stock (page 71) or water
salt and pepper to taste
1 bay leaf

Preheat oven to 350°. In a skillet, heat the oil, and sauté the mushrooms, parsley, onion, and barley. Transfer to a 2-quart casserole along with the stock or water and seasonings. Cover, and bake for 45 minutes, or until the barley is tender and the liquid is absorbed. Serves 4 to 6.

✿ SONIA'S HOMEMADE NOODLES

When slicing the dough, you can make thin, medium or wide noodles, as you desire.

1 egg, beaten　　　　　　*⅔ cup all-purpose flour*
½ teaspoon salt

In a medium bowl, combine all the ingredients. With a big spoon, stir until a dough forms, then moisten your hands, and work the dough by hand until the dough leaves the sides of the bowl and holds together. Form the dough into a ball.

Turn out onto a lightly floured board or counter top, and knead. With a floured rolling pin, roll the dough out in a very thin sheet. Heavily flour one half, fold the unfloured half over, flour again, and roll tightly. Slice the roll into noodles of the width you like. Place the noodles in a strainer, and shake off the excess flour. Allow the noodles to dry for 30 minutes or more, then separate them from each other carefully.

When ready to cook, drop the noodles into rapidly boiling soup or salted water. Cook, stirring often to separate, for 5 to 10 minutes. These noodles can be frozen and kept in the freezer for a month.

For Spinach Noodles: Combine 1 large bunch of fresh spinach with the egg in a blender container, and chop. Place spinach-egg mixture in a bowl and proceed as directed above.

❁────────────────────

BAKED NOODLES

2 *cups milk*	4 *tablespoons sweet butter*
1 *8-ounce package medium*	3 *eggs, separated*
noodles (check the label)	*salt and pepper to taste*

In a saucepan, heat the milk just until boiling. Break the noodles into 1-inch pieces, and cook them in the hot milk until done, about 10 to 12 minutes, over medium heat. Let cool—*do not drain*.

Preheat oven to 350°. Grease a casserole with 1 tablespoon of the butter. Cream the remaining 3 tablespoons butter, and beat in the egg yolks, one at a time. Stir this into the noodle mixture.

In a separate bowl, beat the egg whites until stiff. Fold this into the noodles. Season with salt and pepper.

Bake for 45 minutes, or until lightly browned and an uncolored toothpick inserted in the center comes out clean. Serve directly from the casserole or loosened from the edges and turned out onto a serving dish. Serves 6 to 8.

NOODLE "KOOGEL"

This is good enough to serve as dessert. It serves twelve people. If you need less, bake this recipe in two square pans and freeze one. To reheat after freezing, pour ¼ cup milk evenly over the top.

1 12-ounce package medium noodles (check the label)
6 tablespoons sweet butter
1 3-ounce package cream cheese, softened
½ cup sugar
3 eggs, beaten
1 cup milk
1 cup pear nectar
1 20-ounce can unsweetened crushed pineapple

TOPPING

¼ cup sugar
1 teaspoon ground cinnamon
4 tablespoons sweet butter, softened

Grease a 3-quart rectangular baking dish. Cook the noodles according to package directions; drain well. In a medium saucepan over low heat, melt the butter; mix with the noodles to coat well.

Preheat oven to 350°. In a large bowl, cream together the cheese and sugar. Beat in the eggs, milk, and pear nectar until smooth. Add this mixture to the noodles, and mix together well. Drain the pineapple (if preparing for dessert, reserve the liquid—see Note), and gently stir it into the noodles. Pour the mixture into the baking dish (the mixture will be loose).

To prepare the topping: In a small bowl, beat together all the topping ingredients. Sprinkle over the top of the noodles.

Bake for 1 hour. Let cool to room temperature before cutting and serving. Serves 12.

Note: To prepare a dessert sauce, in a small saucepan over medium heat, heat the reserved pineapple liquid. In a separate bowl, dissolve 1 teaspoon cornstarch in 2 tablespoons of cold water. Add this mixture to the pineapple juice, and cook over medium heat, stirring constantly, until thickened. Serve on the side.

❀————————————————————

NOODLE FRITTERS

1 10-ounce package egg noodles (check the label)
6 tablespoons sweet butter
3 eggs
3 tablespoons milk
1 teaspoon salt

¼ teaspoon pepper
1 teaspoon peeled and grated onion (optional)
solid Crisco shortening for frying

Cook the noodles as directed on the package; drain. Melt the butter, and mix it with the noodles.

In a medium bowl, beat together the eggs, milk, salt, pepper, and onion. Pour this mixture over the noodles, and mix together thoroughly.

Heat a griddle or large skillet, and brush with a light coating of the shortening. Drop the noodle mixture by tablespoonfuls onto the griddle to make 3-inch fritters. Fry over moderate heat until the fritters are browned and crisp on one side; turn, and fry on the other side. Serve immediately. Serves 6.

❀ ────────────────────────

COTTAGE NOODLE PUDDING

*1 8-ounce package noodles
  (check the label)*
4 eggs
1¼ cups milk
*1 cup commercial sour
  cream*

½ pound cottage cheese
¼ cup sugar
¼ cup sweet butter, melted
¾ teaspoon pure vanilla
½ teaspoon salt

Cook the noodles according to the package directions and drain. Preheat oven to 350°. Grease a 2-quart casserole. In a large bowl, mix together all the ingredients until well blended. Pour the mixture into the casserole. Place the casserole in a baking dish, and pour boiling water around the casserole, about 1½ inches deep. Bake for 60 to 75 minutes, or until firm. Can be served either hot or cold. Serves 8.

❀ ────────────────────────

SKILLET MACARONI AND CHEESE

*1 8-ounce package macaroni
  (check the label)*
*1 tablespoon pure vegetable
  oil*
*1 medium onion, peeled and
  thinly sliced (optional)*

*2 tablespoons soy sauce
  (check the label)*
*1 cup grated white Cheddar
  cheese*

In a large saucepan, cook the macaroni according to package directions; drain well. In a large skillet, heat the oil; add the onion if desired, and sauté, turning often, for 5 minutes. Add the macaroni, and cook, stirring until thoroughly heated. Add the soy sauce and grated cheese, mix together well, cover, and steam for a few minutes over low heat until the cheese melts. Serves 6 to 8.

✂————————————————————————————

LASAGNA WITH CHICKEN DOTTIE

⅓ pound uncooked lasagna
  noodles (check the label)
1 teaspoon pure olive oil
4 tablespoons sweet butter,
  melted
¼ cup grated Parmesan
  cheese

1 2½-pound chicken,
  quartered
1 cup fresh mushrooms,
  sliced
2 cups Basic Spaghetti Sauce
  (page 201)

————————————————————————————

Lightly grease a casserole. Cook the lasagna noodles in boiling salted water, to which the olive oil has been added, according to package directions, until tender but not too soft. Drain well. In a large bowl, combine the noodles, 2 tablespoons of the butter, and half the cheese; stir to mix well. Cover the bottom of the casserole with the noodles, bringing them up along the sides of the casserole.

Preheat oven to 425°. In a large, heavy skillet, sauté the chicken quarters in the remaining 2 tablespoons butter, turning, until lightly browned. Cook over medium heat, turning occasionally, for 20 minutes, or until nearly done.

Place the chicken pieces in the lasagna-filled casserole, and pour the cooking juices over them. Arrange the mushrooms over the chicken pieces. Cover with the spaghetti sauce, and sprinkle with the remaining cheese. Bake for 20 minutes, or until warmed through. Serves 4.

❏————————————————————

SPAGHETTI WITH CHICKEN LIVERS AND MUSHROOMS

I 7-ounce package spaghetti
  (check the label)
¾ cup sweet butter
½ pound chicken livers,
  chopped

½ pound fresh mushrooms,
  chopped
½ cup chopped parsley
salt and pepper to taste

————————————————————

Cook the spaghetti according to package directions; drain. In a large skillet over medium heat, melt the butter; add the livers, mushrooms, parsley, and salt and pepper. Cook, stirring frequently, for 5 minutes, or until the mushrooms are tender. Add the spaghetti, and toss everything together. Serve immediately. Serves 4.

❏————————————————————

BASIC SPAGHETTI SAUCE

Here is a sauce especially for Feingolders. We have substituted beets and vinegar for the usual tomato sauce and paste to make a sauce that is truly excellent.

4 tablespoons dried
  mushrooms
3 tablespoons pure olive oil
I pound ground beef
I 16-ounce can diced beets,
  undrained
3 carrots, peeled and diced
3 stalks celery, chopped

2 small onions, peeled and
  finely diced
2 teaspoons white distilled
  vinegar
2 teaspoons mixed Italian
  seasonings
I tablespoon sweet butter

————————————————————

The night before preparing the sauce, wash the dried mushrooms well. Place them in a small bowl, add water, and soak, covered, in the refrigerator overnight. Drain, reserving the liquid, and set aside.

In a large skillet, slowly heat the oil. Brown the meat, breaking it up into very small pieces.

Place the beets with their juice in a blender container, and chop them quite fine, but do not purée. Add the carrots, celery, and onions, and chop well. Add the vegetables to the skillet, and brown lightly. Add the vinegar and seasonings.

Simmer, covered, for 1 hour, stirring occasionally. Stir in the butter, mushrooms, and mushroom liquid, and simmer for 30 minutes longer, stirring occasionally. (The sauce should be thickened by this time.)

Serve hot, over spaghetti, with plenty of Parmesan cheese, served on the side. This sauce is good reheated. Yields 3 cups.

WHITE CLAM SAUCE FOR SPAGHETTI

With a sauce like this one, you won't miss tomato sauce.

*1 10-ounce can whole baby
    clams
3 tablespoons sweet butter
1 clove garlic, peeled and
    minced*

*1 4-ounce can clam juice
⅔ cup chopped parsley
pepper to taste
2½ tablespoons Wondra
    flour*

Drain the clams, reserving the liquid; set aside. In a saucepan, melt the butter. Add the garlic and clams, and simmer for 8 minutes. Stir in the reserved clam liquid, the clam juice, and the parsley, and season with pepper only (clams are salty). Simmer again, gradually adding the flour; cook, stirring, until the sauce has thickened. Serve hot, over spaghetti. Serves 6.

⌘————————————————————

MUSHROOM PASTA SAUCE ANDREA

5 tablespoons pure olive oil
1 pound mushrooms,
  thinly sliced
¼ cup fresh lemon juice

4 green onions, including
  the tops, thinly sliced
  crosswise
salt and pepper to taste

In a heavy skillet, slowly heat the oil. Sauté the mushrooms until soft. Add the lemon juice, onions, and seasonings, and cook over medium heat until thoroughly heated. Serve hot, over buttered pasta. Serves 4.

⌘————————————————————

CHARLOTTE'S PESTO

1 cup pure olive oil
1 clove garlic
2 cups coarsely chopped
  fresh basil

1 cup coarsely chopped
  parsley
1 teaspoon salt
pepper to taste

Place ¼ cup of the oil in a blender container. Peel and dice the garlic, and add it with ½ cup of the basil and ¼ cup of the parsley to the oil; blend until smooth. Add ¼ cup more oil, then another ½ cup basil and ¼ cup parsley; blend again until smooth. Repeat, blending, until all the oil and herbs are used up—the sauce should be thick and green and the consistency of mayonnaise. Season with salt and pepper.

Spoon into a storage jar, and pour a little oil over the top to seal. Store, covered, in the refrigerator. Keeps well for months. Makes 2 cups.

⌘———————————————————

ANDREA'S SALSA VERDE

Serve this green sauce with pasta in place of the conventional tomato sauce.

1 cup chopped spinach
1 cup pure olive oil
½ cup chopped parsley
½ cup grated Parmesan cheese

1 small clove garlic, peeled
1½ tablespoons dried basil
½ teaspoon salt
dash of pepper

———————————————————

Put all the ingredients into a blender container; blend until smooth. To serve, heat in a saucepan over medium heat, and pour over hot, buttered pasta. Stored in a covered jar in the refrigerator, this sauce will keep 1 to 2 weeks. Makes 1½ cups.

❀————————————————————————————

RICE GLAZE FOR HOLIDAY HAM

Most of the glazes used to decorate hams are made with sugar. This is my adaptation of a ham glaze served by Marianne Perry in Brisbane, Australia. It is well worth trying because it is novel, attractive, and sugarless.

*2 tablespoons unflavored
  gelatin
¼ cup cold water
¾ cup hot Kathy's Basic
  Beef or Chicken Stock
  (page 71)*

*2 cups cooked rice
1 red onion, peeled
strips of peel from
  1 zucchini*

————————————————————————————

Sprinkle the gelatin over the water, and let stand for a few minutes. Stir this into the hot stock to dissolve; let cool. Meanwhile, on a platter, cover a cooked ham carefully with the well-separated cooked rice.

When the geletin is thickened and cool, carefully pour it, a tablespoonful at a time, over the rice, patting to keep the rice in place and covering the entire ham.

Cut the red onion pieces to resemble the petals of an iris. Press in place among the rice. Cut the green strips of zucchini peel to look like leaves and stems, and press carefully down into the rice. Cover the "flowers" with additional gelatin. Serve when thoroughly jelled.

SALADS AND
SALAD DRESSINGS

CRUDITÉ SALAD

2 carrots, peeled
4 fresh mushrooms
1 onion, peeled
1 zucchini
watercress for garnish
grated Parmesan cheese

1 3-ounce package cream
  cheese, roughly broken up
2 tablespoons pure olive oil
2 tablespoons dry mustard
1 tablespoon fresh lemon
  juice

Using a vegetable peeler, shave the carrots into paper-thin strips. Slice the mushrooms, onion, and zucchini paper thin. Place the vegetables in a salad bowl, and garnish with watercress. Sprinkle with the Parmesan cheese, and top with the cream cheese.

In a bowl, combine the oil, mustard, and lemon juice. Mix together well. Pour this dressing over the salad, and toss lightly. Serves 4.

LAYERED SALAD

To save time, you can make this easy salad in the morning or the night before, and it will stay perfectly crisp.

¼ head lettuce, shredded
½ small zucchini,
  thinly sliced
½ 10-ounce package frozen
  peas (not defrosted)
½ small can water
  chestnuts, drained and
  thinly sliced
1 stalk celery, thinly sliced

6 small fresh mushrooms,
  thinly sliced
6 radishes, sliced
½ cup homemade
  mayonnaise
  (page 223)
2 tablespoons grated
  Parmesan cheese

Place the shredded lettuce in a serving bowl. Layer each vegetable separately over this, spread with the mayonnaise, and top with the Parmesan cheese. Cover with waxed paper and refrigerate for 8 hours. Serves 6.

❀——————————————

RUTH'S SPINACH AND BEAN SPROUT SALAD

Spinach salad is a fine substitute for the usual lettuce salads.

1 cup fresh bean sprouts
½ pound young spinach
½ cup pure sesame seed oil
or peanut oil
¼ cup soy sauce
(check the label)
2 tablespoons lemon juice
1 small red onion,
peeled and thinly sliced

1½ tablespoons sesame
seeds, lightly toasted
1½ teaspoons sugar
1½ teaspoons pepper
½ cup water chestnuts,
thinly sliced

At least 1 hour before serving, pour enough boiling water over the bean sprouts to cover; let stand for 10 minutes. Drain, and chill. Rinse and dry the spinach well, discard the stems, and chill. In a small bowl, combine the oil, soy sauce, lemon juice, onion, sesame seeds, sugar, and pepper; let stand for 1 hour.

When ready to serve, put the spinach in salad bowl, then layer the bean sprouts and water chestnuts over it. Pour the dressing over all. Serves 6 to 8.

SPINACH AND EGG SALAD WITH YOGURT

4 cups spinach leaves
4 green onions, including 2 inches of the tops, finely chopped
½ cup pure olive oil
1 cup plain, additive-free yogurt
salt and pepper to taste
4 hard-boiled eggs, chopped

Wash the spinach thoroughly. Drain; dry with paper towels. In a salad bowl, shred the spinach, and add the onions. In a separate small bowl, beat the oil, yogurt, and salt and pepper with a fork until well blended. Add the eggs, and pour over the spinach. Toss gently but thoroughly, taking care not to mash the eggs. Cover with waxed paper and refrigerate. Serve chilled. Serves 4.

SUPER CAESAR SALAD

10 tablespoons pure vegetable oil
1 garlic clove, peeled and minced
2 cups bread cubes
1 large head iceberg lettuce, chilled
1 large head romaine lettuce, chilled
¼ cup grated Parmesan cheese
¼ cup crumbled blue cheese
¼ cup lemon juice
¾ teaspoon salt
¼ teaspoon dry mustard
1 egg

In a skillet, heat 2 tablespoons of the oil and the garlic. Add the bread cubes, and sauté until lightly browned. Remove the croutons, and set aside.

Tear the lettuce into bite-sized pieces, and place in a salad bowl. Sprinkle with the Parmesan and blue cheeses. In a jar, combine the remaining 8 tablespoons oil, the lemon juice, salt, and dry mustard, and shake to blend. Pour the dressing over the salad greens, and toss lightly. Break the raw egg into the salad greens, and toss lightly until the egg particles disappear. Add the croutons, and again toss lightly. Serves 6.

✂ ──────────────────────────────

VEGETABLE SALAD DELUXE

Plan to make Pineapple Fluff David (page 298) the same day you make this salad so that you can use up the egg whites this recipe will leave. To save time, you can cook the vegetables a day or two in advance and assemble the salad just before serving.

2 carrots, peeled and sliced
2 new potatoes, peeled and
    diced
1 celery heart, diced; or
    2 stalks celery, sliced
½ pound fresh green beans,
    sliced
1 pound fresh peas or
    ½ pound frozen peas
¼ pound fresh mushrooms
juice of 1 lemon

2 egg yolks
1 teaspoon dry mustard
salt and pepper to taste
½ cup pure olive oil
¼ cup white distilled vinegar
2 tablespoons chopped
    chives
1 sprig parsley, chopped
dash of tarragon
dash of paprika

In a large saucepan, combine the carrots, potatoes, celery, and beans; add just enough water to cover. Boil until almost cooked—about 20 minutes. Add the peas, and cook for a few minutes longer, or just until done—do not overcook. Drain, reserving the liquid, and chill. (The reserved liquid can be used to make soup.)

When ready to serve, wash and slice the mushrooms, and sprinkle them with lemon juice. Let stand. In a small bowl mix the egg yolks with the mustard, salt, pepper, oil and vinegar to make a dressing, and pour this over the cooked vegetables in a large serving bowl. Add the mushrooms, chives, parsley and paprika. Serve with cold meats.

✿ SAN DIEGO COLESLAW

This is another San Diego Feingold Association recipe.

½ head cabbage, shredded
3 tablespoons homemade
  mayonnaise
  (page 223)

¼ cup permitted fruit juice,
  such as pineapple,
  grapefruit, pear, guava, or
  papaya

At least 1 hour before serving, in a small bowl, combine the fruit juice and mayonnaise. Pour this over the cabbage, and toss to mix. Refrigerate until ready to serve. Serves 4.

✿ COLESLAW

1 cup cold commercial
  sour cream
¼ cup honey

2 teaspoons celery seeds
1 teaspoon salt
4 cups shredded cabbage

In a small bowl, beat the sour cream well, and add the next three ingredients. Pour this dressing over the cabbage, and mix. Serves 8.

✠ CARROT-ZUCCHINI SLAW

1 large carrot
2 medium zucchini
2 tablespoons pure vegetable oil

1 tablespoon lemon juice
1 teaspoon celery seeds
1 teaspoon dry mustard
salt and pepper to taste

The day before serving, wash, pare, and shred the carrot and zucchini. Keep in separate, covered bowls in the refrigerator overnight. About 4 hours before serving, mix together the remaining ingredients. Combine the vegetables, pour over the sauce, and toss all together. Cover, and chill until serving time. Serves 6.

✠ CARROT AND CAULIFLOWER SLAW

1 small head cauliflower
4 carrots, peeled and thinly sliced
¼ cup pure vegetable or olive oil

2 tablespoons white distilled vinegar
2 tablespoons homemade mustard (page 158)
1 teaspoon sugar

Wash the cauliflower, separate it into flowerets, and cut these into ¼-inch slices.

In a medium saucepan, bring a small amount of salted water to a boil; add the carrots, cover, and cook for 5 minutes. Add the cauliflower, and cook for an addiitonal 5 minutes. Remove from heat.

In a small bowl, combine the oil, vinegar, mustard, and sugar. Pour this over the vegetables, and toss lightly. Chill thoroughly. Serves 4 to 6.

SUMMER SALAD

3 medium bananas,
  peeled and sliced
1 guava, peeled and diced
1 grapefruit, sectioned and
  diced
1 cup pineapple, peeled and
  diced
½ cup unsalted sunflower
  seeds

½ cup walnuts
½ cup plain, additive-free
  yogurt
1 tablespoon honey
1 tablespoon unsweetened
  pineapple juice
¼ cup unsweetened
  shredded coconut

Combine all the fruits in a serving bowl. Add the sunflower seeds and walnuts. In a separate bowl, combine the yogurt, honey, and pineapple juice. Pour this dressing over the fruit. Toss, and mix together well. Garnish with shredded coconut. Serves 6 to 8.

GRAPEFRUIT-AVOCADO SALAD

A refreshing salad for everyone in the family.

1 tablespoon unflavored gelatin
¼ cup cold water
1 cup hot water
1 3-ounce package cream cheese, softened

1 cup grapefruit sections, diced
4 tablespoons lemon juice
¼ cup sugar
½ teaspoon salt
1 avocado, peeled and diced

Grease well a 4-cup ring mold. In a medium bowl, sprinkle the gelatin over the cold water, and dissolve; let stand for a few minutes. Pour in the hot water, and mix thoroughly; let cool.

Meanwhile, in a small bowl, mash the cream cheese with a fork. When the gelatin is cool, stir in the mashed cheese, grapefruit, lemon juice, sugar, salt, and avocado. Spoon into the ring mold. Refrigerate for 6 hours, or until set. Serves 4 to 6.

NAOMI'S AUSTRALIAN RICE SALAD

In Adelaide, Australia, rice salad is served with cold meats and vegetable salads at most evening meals. This is a good use for leftover rice.

1 cup cooked rice, chilled
1 onion, peeled and
   finely chopped
2 tablespoons finely chopped
   parsley

¼ cup pure vegetable oil
2 tablespoons white distilled
   vinegar
½ teaspoon sugar
½ teaspoon curry powder
salt and pepper to taste

Mix all the ingredients together well. Chill and serve. Makes 1 cup.

✄ CAROL CUMMINGS' POTATO SALAD

8 to 10 small potatoes
½ small onion, peeled and
   chopped
salt and pepper to taste
¼ cup white distilled vinegar

½ pint sour cream
3 tablespoons homemade
   mayonnaise (page 223)
¼ cup milk

Boil the potatoes until soft when tested with a fork, about 25 minutes. Peel, slice and season with salt and pepper. Add the onion and vinegar, and let stand for about 30 minutes. Mix the sour cream, mayonnaise and milk together. Add the potatoes and onion and mix well. Serve warm or chilled. Serves 8.

HENNIE'S POTATO SALAD

Though this may not be the easiest salad to make, it is by far the very best to eat. What makes it difficult is that the potatoes must be peeled and sliced while hot. Hold them with a clean towel or pot holder for protection.

4 *medium White Rose potatoes*	6 *small sprigs parsley, finely chopped*
2 *small onions, peeled and sliced*	⅓ *cup white distilled vinegar*
	½ *teaspoon salt*
⅔ *cup pure olive oil*	¼ *teaspoon pepper*

Boil the potatoes with their skins on until just tender but not soft. While they are still hot, peel and slice them. In the bottom of a large serving bowl, layer the slices of one potato. Cover with about one-quarter of the onion slices and parsley. Pour one-quarter of the oil, then one-quarter of vinegar over them. Season with the salt and pepper, and repeat the layers, beginning with potato slices, until all the ingredients are used up.

Stir gently with a fork or wooden spoon until the potatoes are well coated. Serve warm. (If refrigerated, bring to room temperature, and stir gently.) Serves 4.

HOT CHICKEN SALAD

An excellent luncheon dish, most of this salad can be made a day in advance—just add the cheese and potato chips right before baking and serve as soon as the cheese melts. You can add ½ cup of chopped peanuts to the salad if you like.

1 cup homemade
  mayonnaise (page 223)
2 cups cubed cooked chicken
2 cups finely chopped celery
½ small onion, peeled and
  grated

juice of ½ lemon
½ cup shredded white
  American cheese
1 cup crushed pure potato
  chips
dash of paprika

Preheat oven to 350°. Lightly grease a baking dish with 1 tablespoon of the mayonnaise.

In a large bowl, mix together the chicken, celery, onion, lemon juice, and the remaining mayonnaise. Pour the mixture into the baking dish. Sprinkle with the cheese, potato chips, and paprika. Bake for 15 to 20 minutes, or until the mixture is heated through and the cheese has melted. Serves 4.

BETTY'S TEXAS TACO SALAD

This salad is great for a teen-ager's supper party or for a buffet. If you like tacos, you'll enjoy this variation.

1 pound ground beef
1 15½-ounce can red kidney
  beans, drained
2 avocados, peeled and
  cut into bite-sized pieces
1 cup diced celery
1 cup pitted black olives
½ cup green salad olives
½ cup white Cheddar
  cheese, cut into small
  strips

1 4-ounce can mushrooms,
  drained
dash of soy sauce
  (check the label)
½ head lettuce, torn into
  bite-sized pieces
1 6-ounce package pure
  tortilla chips
Basic French Dressing
  (page 224)

Heat a skillet, and brown the meat in it. Drain off excess fat, let cool, and refrigerate.

In a large bowl, mix together the remaining ingredients, except for the lettuce, tortilla chips, and salad dressing. Add the meat to the mixture, and chill. Just before serving, add the lettuce and chips. Serve with homemade salad dressing on the side. Serves 4 to 6.

✖————————————————————————

CURRIED TUNA SALAD ROZ

When using chutney, be sure it is made with permitted fruits. Mango chutney is the most popular and is easily available.

2 7-ounce cans tuna, drained
3 cups cold cooked rice
2 cups chopped celery
1 10-ounce package frozen
mixed vegetables, cooked,
drained, and cooled
½ cup Basic French
Dressing (page 224)

½ cup chutney, chopped
(check the label)
¼–½ teaspoon curry
powder, to taste
lettuce

Early in the day, in a large mixing bowl, toss all the ingredients except lettuce until well mixed. Cover, and refrigerate. At serving time, line a salad bowl with lettuce. Toss the tuna mixture again, and spoon it into the lettuce-lined salad bowl. Serves 6.

SALMON MOLD MARION

In Brisbane, Australia, this dish was molded in avocado halves for a spectacular salad at a buffet dinner. Smaller amounts would be an ideal first course at any dinner.

2 8-ounce cans salmon,
  drained
2 tablespoons unflavored
  gelatin
1 8-ounce package cream
  cheese, softened

1 cup chopped celery
1 onion, peeled and diced
2 cups homemade
  mayonnaise (page 223)

Place all the ingredients in a blender container, and blend until smooth. (If pink salmon is used, color with a few drops of beet juice.) Pour the mixture into a mold. Cover with waxed paper and place in the refrigerator to set, several hours or overnight. Serves 8 or more.

HERRING SALAD

This is a Russian version of herring salad with sour cream.

4 boiled beets, peeled and
  diced
4 boiled potatoes, peeled and
  diced
2 tablespoons finely chopped
  onion or green onion
1 teaspoon sugar
3 tablespoons white distilled
  vinegar

1 8-ounce jar herring filets
1½ cups commercial sour
  cream
2 hard-broiled eggs
2 teaspoons chopped parsley
½ teaspoon dried dillweed
dash of white pepper
small pinch of salt

In a large bowl, mix together the beets and potatoes. In a separate bowl, mix the onion with the sugar and vinegar; stir this into the vegetables.

Cut the herring into small pieces. Just before serving, mix it together with the sour cream and vegetables. Pour the mixture into a serving dish, and garnish with the eggs, parsley, dillweed, and pepper. Sprinkle a very little salt on top. Serves 6.

CARLA'S HERRING SALAD

Prepare this a day or two in advance to get the full flavor. It is a typical German-style herring salad. If apples are permitted, add one tart apple, finely chopped.

1 16-ounce can red beets, drained and finely chopped

2 potatoes, boiled but not soft, finely chopped

1 8-ounce jar marinated herring, cut into small pieces

1 small onion, peeled and chopped

1 tablespoon white distilled vinegar

1 teaspoon brown sugar

2 tablespoons homemade mayonnaise (page 223)

1 hard-boiled egg, chopped or put through a sieve

1 teaspoon capers

In a large bowl, mix the beets, potatoes, herring, onion, vinegar, and brown sugar. Cover, and refrigerate for at least 24 hours.

Just before serving, add enough mayonnaise to the mixture to bind the vegetables together. Garnish with the egg and capers. Serves 6 to 8.

✂——————————————————————————

MAYONNAISE FROM GRANDMA'S KITCHEN

Use pure olive oil for a distinctive flavor, or a pure vegetable oil for everyday use.

2 eggs
1 teaspoon salt
½ teaspoon dry mustard
¼ teaspoon paprika
2 tablespoons white distilled
*   vinegar*

2 cups pure vegetable or
*   olive oil*
2 tablespoons lemon juice
1 tablespoon hot water

——————————————————————————

Place the eggs, salt, mustard, and paprika in a blender container; blend for about 30 seconds. Add the vinegar, and blend until smooth. While the blender is running, gradually add 1½ cups of the oil in a slow, steady stream. When very well blended, carefully add the remaining ½ cup oil and the lemon juice alternately, both in a steady stream, until everything is completely mixed. Lastly, add the hot water 2 drops at a time, and blend for a smooth consistency. Spoon the mayonnaise into a storage container, cover, and refrigerate until ready to use. Makes 2½ cups.

✂——————————————————————————

BLENDER MAYONNAISE

1 egg
5 teaspoons lemon juice
1 teaspoon dry mustard
¾ teaspoon salt

¼ teaspoon white pepper
1 cup pure olive or
*   vegetable oil*

——————————————————————————

In a blender container, combine the egg, lemon juice, mustard, salt, and pepper; blend on high speed until the mixture is thick and lemon colored. Continue blending, adding the oil very gradually in a thin, steady stream. (If the mayonnaise is too thick, add 1 tablespoon of warm water.) Refrigerate, covered, until ready to use. Makes 1¼ cups.

❀ BASIC FRENCH DRESSING

If you do not find mixed Italian seasonings on your grocer's spice shelves, you can make some yourself using a teaspoon each of rosemary, oregano, savory, thyme, marjoram, sage, and basil. Crumble all together very well, and store in a glass container.

1 cup pure vegetable or olive oil
⅓ cup white distilled vinegar or lemon juice
½ teaspoon salt
1 teaspoon dry mustard

1 teaspoon peeled and grated onion
¼ teaspoon mixed Italian seasonings
½ teaspoon paprika

In a shaker or jar with a tight-fitting lid, mix the ingredients together well. Chill. Store in the refrigerator, and shake well before using. Makes 1⅓ cups.

❀————————————————————

LEMON-OIL DRESSING

This is one of the recipes from the San Diego Survival Handbook that help during those first four weeks on the Feingold Diet.

¼ cup lemon juice
1 tablespoon pure vegetable
   or olive oil

1 teaspoon salt
1 clove garlic, peeled and
   crushed

In a jar with a tight-fitting lid, combine all the ingredients, and shake until well mixed. Refrigerate, covered, until ready to use. Makes ¼ cup.

❀————————————————————

YOGURT-OLIVE DRESSING

Serve this with salad greens for a delicious salad, or try it as a dip with raw vegetables and cooked string beans.

⅓ cup homemade
   mayonnaise (page 223)
2 tablespoons finely chopped
   green or black olives
2 tablespoons peeled and
   chopped onion

⅛ teaspoon garlic powder
½ teaspoon sugar
1 cup plain, additive-free
   yogurt

In a small bowl, mix the mayonnaise with the olives, onion, garlic powder, and sugar. Fold in the yogurt. Cover, and chill until ready to serve. Makes 1½ cups.

PAPAYA-SEED DRESSING

Excellent on tossed greens or on fruit salads, this dressing makes use of saved papaya seeds.

⅓ cup sugar
1 teaspoon salt
1 teaspoon dry mustard
½ cup white distilled
   vinegar

1 cup pure vegetable oil
1 small onion, peeled and
   chopped
3 tablespoons papaya seeds

Place the sugar, salt, dry mustard, and vinegar in a blender container. Blend, gradually adding the oil, then the onion. When thoroughly mixed, add the papaya seeds, blending only until the seeds are the size of coarsely ground pepper. Makes 1⅔ cups.

DRESSING FOR FRUIT SALAD

Because of the celery seeds this dressing has a piquant flavor.

¼ cup sugar
1 teaspoon dry mustard
1 teaspoon salt
¼ onion, peeled and grated

⅓ cup white distilled
   vinegar
1 cup pure vegetable oil
1 tablespoon celery seeds

Into a small bowl, place the sugar, mustard, and salt; add the onion and a small amount of the vinegar. Stir, gradually adding the oil, the remainder of the vinegar, and the celery seeds. Refrigerate, covered, until ready to serve. Serve over any combination of fruits, with Cottage Cheese Ring (page 234) sliced avocado, or sectioned grapefruit. Makes 1½ cups.

❁────────────────────────────

CREAMY BLUE CHEESE FREEZE

This is novel for a summer salad. Serve it cut into squares or molded in small muffin tins, with marinated artichoke hearts or homemade French dressing on the side, or with fruit salads.

¼ pound blue cheese,
  softened
salt and pepper to taste

1 cup heavy cream,
  beaten stiff

In a medium bowl, cream the blue cheese until smooth. Add the salt and pepper. Fold in the stiffly beaten cream. Place the mixture in slightly oiled muffin tins or refrigerator ice cube trays covered with waxed paper. Freeze overnight or until firm. Serves 8.

EGGS AND CHEESE

JEN'S SCRAMBLED EGGS

2 eggs   2 tablespoons cottage cheese
1 tablespoon sweet butter

In a bowl, beat the eggs well. In a small skillet over medium heat, melt the butter, and add the beaten eggs. As soon as the edges of the eggs set, add the cottage cheese, and scramble the mixture, stirring constantly, until the eggs are thick but still creamy. Serves 1.

SCRAMBLED CREAM-CHEESE EGGS

6 eggs   1 teaspoon salt
½ cup light cream   dash of pepper
1 3-ounce package cream   2 tablespoons sweet butter
   cheese, quartered

Place all the ingredients except for the butter in a blender container. Blend on medium speed for 10 seconds. In a skillet over medium heat, heat the butter. Pour the egg mixture into the hot skillet, and cook, stirring constantly, until the eggs are thick but still creamy. Serves 4 to 6.

EGGS IN A BASKET

4 slices French bread,
about ½ inch thick

4 tablespoons sweet butter
4 eggs

Remove a half-dollar size piece from the center of each slice of bread. Grease a skillet, and slowly heat. Butter the bread on both sides. Fry the bread slices on one side until lightly browned—about 2 minutes. Turn the slices, and break an egg into the center of each one; fry the egg and bread together. Serves 2 to 4.

BAKED EGGS AND CHEESE

1 tablespoon sweet butter
6 ounces white Cheddar
cheese, crumbled
6 eggs

salt to taste
1 cup commercial sour
cream
¼ cup milk

Preheat oven to 325°. Grease 6 small ramekins or custard cups with ½ teaspoon butter each. Into each cup sprinkle 1 ounce of the cheese. Break an egg over the cheese, and season to taste.

In a small bowl, beat together the sour cream and milk. Spoon this mixture over the eggs. Bake for 15 to 20 minutes, depending on the desired firmness of the egg yolk. Serves 6.

❁————————————————

PARTY DEVILED EGGS

Before stuffing the whites, you can color them by soaking them in red beet juice, an especially attractive garnish for the Easter ham.

6 eggs
1 tablespoon homemade
    mayonnaise (page 223)
1½ teaspoons white distilled
    vinegar

¼ teaspoon homemade
    mustard (page 158)
¼ teaspoon salt
¼ cup whipped cream or
    commercial sour cream

Boil the eggs until very hard—about 20 minutes; shell them, and let them cool completely. Halve the eggs lengthwise, and remove the yolks to a medium bowl, being careful not to break the egg whites; reserve the egg whites. Mash the yolks, or press them through a sieve. Add the remaining ingredients, and mix with a fork until smooth and fluffy. Mound the yolk mixture back into the egg white centers.

❁————————————————

EGG FOO YONG

½ cup finely chopped
    cooked pork
½ cup peeled and
    finely chopped onion
¼ cup thinly sliced water
    chestnuts

1 cup bean sprouts
6 eggs, well beaten
¼ teaspoon salt
pure vegetable or
    sesame oil for frying

In a large bowl, mix together the pork, onion, water chestnuts, and bean sprouts with a fork. Add the eggs and salt to the pork mixture, and beat until thick.

In a skillet over medium heat, heat 1 inch of the oil. Ladle enough egg mixture into the pan to make round pancakes, 4 inches in diameter. Fry for about 10 minutes, or until the underside is browned; turn, and brown the other side. Drain well on paper towels. Serve with soy sauce on the side. (Check the label.) Serves 6.

✂———————————————————

COTTAGE CHEESE RING

This can be made with or without whipped cream. Without, serve with avocados. With, serve with pears, pineapple, or papaya. Either way, serve it with the Dressing for Fruit Salad (page 226).

*2 tablespoons unflavored
  gelatin
¼ cup cold water
1 cup hot milk*

*pinch of salt
4 cups cottage cheese
1 cup whipped cream
  (optional)*

———————————————————————

Grease a ring mold. In a medium bowl, sprinkle the gelatin over the water; let stand for a few minutes. Pour the hot milk over the gelatin, and stir to dissolve. Add the salt.

When the gelatin mixture has cooled, add the cottage cheese and whipped cream, and stir until well mixed. Pour into the mold, and chill for 4 hours. Serves 10 to 12.

✿ LUNCHEON SANDWICHES

For a birthday luncheon, these sandwiches will delight children and parents. Trim off the crusts and cut in quarters to serve as an appetizer.

8 slices mozzarella cheese
8 slices pure white bread
2 eggs, slightly beaten

½ cup milk
salt and pepper to taste
4 tablespoons sweet butter

Place 2 slices of cheese each on 4 slices of bread, and cover with another bread slice.

In a medium bowl, beat the eggs with the milk and seasonings. Carefully dip the sandwiches into the mixture so that both pieces of bread are coated.

In a skillet, heat the butter and fry the sandwiches on both sides. Makes 4 sandwiches.

✿ TOASTY CHEESE BAKE

8 slices pure bread
4 tablespoons sweet butter
¼ cup peeled and
  chopped onion
½ pound ground beef
1 tablespoon homemade
  mustard (page 158)

2 tablespoons chopped celery
1 teaspoon salt
¾ cup milk
1 cup grated white Cheddar
  cheese
¼ teaspoon pepper
⅛ teaspoon dry mustard

Toast the bread slices, and butter both sides. In a skillet, combine the onion with the ground beef, mustard, celery, and ½ teaspoon of the salt. Cook, stirring, until the meat browns and the onion is tender.

Preheat oven to 350°. Grease a 9-by-9-by-2-inch pan. In a small bowl, mix together the milk and cheese. Arrange 4 pieces of the toast in the pan; layer half the meat mixture over, and top with half the cheese mixture. Repeat the layering. Sprinkle with the remaining ½ teaspoon salt, the pepper, and the dry mustard, and bake, uncovered, for 30 to 35 minutes. Serves 4 to 6.

BREADS

This recipe, from Albany, New York, is ideal because the sugar content is low—the dates supply the sugar usually found in nut breads. Serve it with cream cheese as an afternoon snack.

1 cup pitted dates, chopped
1 cup water
3 tablespoons sweet butter,
   softened
⅓ cup honey
2 eggs
½ teaspoon pure vanilla
1½ cups whole-wheat flour

2 teaspoons baking powder
½ teaspoon ground
   cinnamon
¼ teaspoon salt
½ cup milk
¾ cup chopped nuts
   (any except almonds)

Preheat oven to 325°. Grease a loaf pan.

Bring the water to a boil; add the dates, and boil, stirring, until a thick mixture is formed.

In a large bowl, cream the butter; add the honey, and blend well. Beat in the eggs and vanilla until well mixed. In a separate bowl, mix together the flour, baking powder, cinnamon, and salt.

Beginning and ending with the flour mixture, beat in one-fourth of the flour alternately with one-third of the milk. Stir in the dates and nuts. Pour the mixture into the loaf pan, and bake for 1¼ hours, or until an uncolored toothpick inserted in the center comes out clean. Cool before serving. Makes 1 loaf.

✿ NUT BREAD

4 cups all-purpose flour
4 teaspoons baking powder
⅓ cup sugar
1 teaspoon salt

1 egg
2 cups milk
1 cup walnuts, chopped

Grease a loaf pan. In a large mixing bowl, sift together the dry ingredients. In a separate bowl, beat the egg with the milk; beat this into the dry ingredients. Fold in the chopped nuts. Cover, and let rise in a warm place for 30 minutes.

Preheat oven to 350°. Pour the dough into the loaf pan, and bake for 45 minutes, or until an uncolored toothpick inserted in the center comes out clean. Cool before serving. Makes 1 loaf.

✿ ANDREA'S QUICK PINEAPPLE BREAD

This recipe makes three medium loaves, freezes well, and, like other fruit breads, can be served as a dessert.

3 cups unbleached white
   flour
½ teaspoon salt
2 teaspoons baking powder
1 teaspoon baking soda
⅔ cup solid Crisco
   shortening

1⅓ cups sugar
½ cup milk
1½ teaspoons lemon juice
4 eggs
1 cup unsweetened crushed
   pineapple, drained

Preheat oven to 350°. Grease and flour three loaf pans. Sift the flour together with the salt, baking powder, and baking soda; set aside.

In a large bowl, cream the shortening until light; gradually beat in the sugar, milk, lemon juice, eggs, and pineapple. Stir in the dry ingredients, beating by hand until well mixed.

Pour the mixture into loaf pans; bake for 40 to 45 minutes, or until an uncolored toothpick inserted in the center comes out clean. Remove from the pans, and cool. Makes 3 loaves.

⌘————————————

LEMON BREAD

This bread hails from British Columbia. The lemony taste is refreshing.

rinds of 3 lemons	*¾ cup milk*
1 cup sugar	*1 teaspoon pure vanilla*
½ cup water	*¼ cup solid Crisco*
2 cups all-purpose flour	*shortening, melted*
4 teaspoons baking powder	*½ cup walnuts, chopped*
½ teaspoon salt	*½ cup pitted dates, chopped*

Cut the lemon rind in thin strips. Put in a small saucepan and cover with water; simmer until tender—about 15 minutes. Drain.

Preheat oven to 350°. Grease a loaf pan well.

In a medium saucepan, combine the cooked rind, the sugar, and the water. Simmer over low heat, stirring constantly, until the liquid thickens and coats the spoon. Cool.

In a large bowl, sift together the flour, baking powder, and salt. At low speed or by hand, beat in the rind syrup, milk, vanilla, and melted shortening. Stir in the nuts and dates, and pour the mixture into the loaf pan. Bake for 1 hour. Cool. Makes 1 loaf.

NOT-SO-IRISH SODA BREAD

While this bread is made with soda, it also contains not-very-traditional whole-wheat flour and yogurt.

2 cups whole-wheat flour
½ teaspoon salt
1 teaspoon baking soda
1 tablespoon honey
1 cup plain, additive-free yogurt or buttermilk
1 egg, beaten

Preheat oven to 375°. Grease a baking sheet. In a large bowl, stir the dry ingredients together. In a separate bowl, beat the honey and yogurt into the beaten egg. Gradually pour the liquids into the dry ingredients, blending by hand. Knead in the bowl or on a bread board for about 5 minutes.

Shape into a round, flat loaf, and place it on the baking sheet. Cut two parallel slashes into the dough, about ½ inch deep. Bake for 25 to 30 minutes. Makes 1 loaf.

FRENCH BREAD WITH CAMEMBERT

This is a bread recipe that is excellent reheated.

4 ounces Camembert cheese
½ teaspoon Charlotte's Pesto (page 203)
½ teaspoon onion salt
½ cup sweet butter
1 loaf French bread

In a medium saucepan over low heat, combine the first four ingredients. Simmer, stirring constantly, until blended— about 5 minutes. Remove from heat, and cool, stirring occasionally, until the mixture starts to thicken—about 10 minutes.

Meanwhile, preheat oven to 325°. Slice the bread in half lengthwise. Spread the cheese mixture on the cut surfaces of bread; put the loaf together again, and spread whatever cheese mixture remains over the top and sides of the loaf. Wrap the loaf in foil; bake for 20 minutes. Open the foil at the top, and bake for 5 minutes longer, or until the crust is browned. Makes 12 servings.

✣——————————

MEXICAN BREAD

These squares turn out to be light, flaky, and like a puff paste.

1 cup Homemade Biscuit *¼ cup water*
  Mix (page 248) *pure vegetable oil for frying*

Place the biscuit mix in a medium bowl. Very gradually beat in the water to make a soft but not sticky dough. Turn out onto a floured bread board, and knead well—about 5 minutes. Let stand in a warm place, covered with a towel, for 30 minutes.

In a deep-fat fryer or electric fryer, slowly heat 1½ to 2 inches of the oil to 375°. With a floured rolling pin, roll out the dough ⅛ inch thick. Cut into 2½-inch squares. Fry the squares for about 5 minutes, or until golden brown. Lift them out with a slotted spoon, and drain on paper towels. Serve at once. Makes 12 squares.

❦————————————————————————

HINT O' HONEY LOAVES

2 cubes fresh yeast
½ cup very warm water
2¼ cups milk, scalded
⅓ cup honey
¼ cup sweet butter
2½ teaspoons salt

6–6½ cups unbleached,
  unsifted, white flour
2 cups uncooked rolled oats
2 tablespoons sweet butter,
  melted

————————————————————————

Place the yeast cubes in the water, and let stand for 5 minutes to dissolve.

In a large bowl, pour the scalded milk over the honey, butter, and salt, stirring until the butter melts; cool to lukewarm. Add 2 cups of the flour, all the oats, and the dissolved yeast; mix together well. With a wooden spoon, stir in enough of the remaining flour to make a soft dough.

Grease a large bowl. Turn the dough out onto a lightly floured board. Knead for about 8 to 10 minutes, or until the dough is smooth and elastic. Shape the dough into a ball, and place it in the greased bowl, turning to coat the surface of the dough. Cover with a damp cloth. Let the dough rise in a warm place until doubled in size, about 1 hour. Punch down the dough; cover with a damp cloth, and let rest for 10 minutes.

Grease two 9-by-5-inch loaf pans. Shape the dough to form two loaves, and place them in the pans. Brush with the melted butter. Cover again with a damp cloth, and let the loaves rise for about 45 minutes, or until nearly doubled in size.

Just before the rising time is completed, preheat oven to 350°. Bake the loaves for about 45 minutes, or until they sound hollow when thumped with your knuckles. Turn them out of the pans, and cool on wire racks. Makes 2 loaves.

244

EAST AFRICAN WHOLE WHEAT BREAD

1 cube fresh yeast
1½ cups warm water
  (105° to 115°)
2 tablespoons honey
2 tablespoons pure vegetable
  oil

2 cups whole-wheat flour
2½ cups all-purpose flour
1 tablespoon salt

In a large bowl, place the yeast cubes in ¼ cup of very warm water, and let stand for 5 minutes to dissolve. Stir in the honey; when frothy stir in the oil, the whole-wheat flour, 2 cups of the all-purpose flour, the salt, and 1¼ cups of warm water. Knead the dough in the bowl for a minute or two.

Flour a board with the remaining ½ cup all-purpose flour. Turn the dough out onto it, and knead for about 10 minutes, or until the dough is smooth and silky.

Grease a large bowl. Shape the dough into a ball, and place it in the greased bowl, turning to coat the surface of the dough. Cover with a kitchen towel, and let rise in a warm spot until doubled in bulk.

Divide the dough into three equal parts. Roll each third into a ball. Pat (do not roll) each ball into a ½-inch-thick circle, and place it on an ungreased baking sheet. Let rise again until doubled in size. (Dough will be mounded in the center when risen—it takes 30 minutes or more.)

Just before rising is completed, preheat oven to 375°. Bake for 35 to 40 minutes, or until the bread makes a hollow sound when thumped. Cool to just warm before serving. Makes 3 loaves.

❆————————————————

CROUTONS BY CLEO

Use these in salads, soups, or for savory snacks. If you make them at home from pure bread, you'll know they contain no preservatives.

With a sharp knife, cut off the crusts from bread slices, and reserve them for Cleo Jeppson's Bread Crumbs (page 262). Butter the bread on one side. Arrange the slices in a single layer, butter side up, on an ungreased baking sheet. Freeze until firm—about 1 hour.

When frozen, cut with a sharp knife or kitchen shears into ½-inch squares. (You can save time by stacking a few at a time before cutting.)

Preheat oven to 300°. Spread or toss the squares on the baking sheet, and bake, stirring occasionally, until the croutons are lightly toasted—about 20 to 25 minutes. Remove them from the oven, and let stand until they are completely dry and crisp. Can be stored in paper bags for several days.

❆————————————————

YEAST DOUGH FOR COFFEE CAKE

This makes a good coffee cake, light in texture and with little sugar. It will make eight dozen pecan or cinnamon rolls, four large coffee cakes, or four dozen sweet rolls.

4 cubes fresh yeast
1 cup very warm water
½ cup sugar
1 teaspoon salt
½ cup cold milk
1 cup commercial sour
   cream

2 teaspoons lemon juice
1 teaspoon pure vanilla
3 egg yolks
5–6 cups all-purpose flour
1½ cups sweet butter,
   softened

In a medium bowl, place the yeast cubes in the water. Add the sugar, and let stand for 5 minutes to dissolve. Stir in the salt, milk, sour cream, lemon juice, vanilla, egg yolks, and enough of the flour to make a medium-firm dough.

In a bowl or on a bread board, knead the softened butter into the dough until it is smooth and elastic (about 10 minutes), adding more flour if necessary. Cover the bowl with waxed paper and refrigerate for at least 4 hours, punching it down every hour, until thoroughly chilled. Use for Pecan Rolls for Feingold Parties (below). Store only overnight.

PECAN ROLLS FOR FEINGOLD PARTIES

1½ cups firmly packed
   brown sugar
⅓ cup honey
96 whole pecans, about 1 cup
1 recipe Yeast Dough for
   Coffee Cake (above)

4 teaspoons ground
   cinnamon
½ cup pecans,
   finely chopped

Preheat oven to 375°. Generously grease 8 dozen tiny muffin cups. Place ¼ teaspoon brown sugar, a drop of honey, and 1 pecan in the bottom of each muffin cup.

Divide the coffee cake dough into eight equal parts. On a floured board or counter top, roll each part into a rectangle. Sprinkle each dough rectangle with 1 tablespoon brown sugar, ½ teaspoon cinnamon, and 1 tablespoon finely chopped pecans. Roll the rectangles tightly, jelly-roll style, sealing the seams with a little cold water. Slice the rolls into ¾-inch pieces (to fill each muffin cup two-thirds full) and press the dough firmly into the cups.

Cover with waxed paper and a kitchen towel. Let rise for 20 minutes, or until the dough looks puffy. Bake for 20 minutes, or until golden. Immediately turn the rolls out of the muffin cups and onto waxed paper or a counter top. Let the glaze run down the sides. Makes 96 rolls.

✿ HOMEMADE BISCUIT MIX

Many recipes in this book call for the use of this mix, which came from Vernon, British Columbia. Keep it on hand to use in a variety of ways and to simplify your baking.

10 cups all-purpose flour
⅓ cup baking powder
1 tablespoon salt

2 cups solid Crisco
   shortening

In a very large bowl, mix the dry ingredients together. With a pastry blender or by hand, cut in the shortening until the mixture resembles coarse meal. Store the mix in a closed container in the refrigerator—it will keep for several months.

To prepare biscuits: Preheat oven to 450°. For every 5 to 6 biscuits you need, mix 1 cup of the biscuit mix with ¼ cup milk. On a floured board, roll out the dough ½ inch thick, and cut out biscuits to the desired size. (Do not pack the mixture when measuring. Measure lightly.) Place on an ungreased baking sheet, and bake for 8 to 10 minutes.

❁————————————————————

ANGEL-FLAKE BISCUITS

If you've always wanted to make a Southern biscuit, here is the perfect recipe, thanks to Gerrie of Baytown, Texas. Note that a buttermilk substitute can be made by putting 2⅔ tablespoons white distilled vinegar in a large measuring cup and then filling to the 2-cup line with regular milk.

1 cube fresh yeast	*3 tablespoons baking powder*
¼ cup very warm water	*3 tablespoons sugar*
5 cups all-purpose flour	*¾ cup solid Crisco*
1 teaspoon salt	*shortening*
½ teaspoon baking soda	*2 cups buttermilk*

Place the yeast cube in the water, and let stand for 5 minutes to dissolve.

In a large bowl, stir together the flour, salt, baking soda, baking powder, and sugar. By hand or with a pastry blender, cut the shortening into the mixture. Add the dissolved yeast and the buttermilk, and mix together well. Refrigerate in a tightly closed plastic bag—the dough will keep for 5 days.

To bake biscuits: Preheat oven to 450°. Grease a baking pan. Cut off the amount of dough needed. With a rolling pin roll the dough thin, folding it several times. Roll it finally to ½-inch thickness, and cut out biscuits to the desired size. Place the biscuits in the pan, and bake at once (do not let rise before cooking) for 12 minutes. Makes 24 biscuits.

NO-KNEAD REFRIGERATOR ROLLS

This dough, covered with a damp cloth, can be kept in the refrigerator and used as needed for up to three days. Punch down occasionally, and keep the cloth damp.

2 *cubes fresh yeast*
2 *cups very warm water*
(105° to 115°)
½ *cup sugar*
1½ *teaspoons salt*

7 *cups all-purpose flour*
1 *egg*
¼ *cup solid Crisco*
shortening

In a large bowl, place the yeast in the water, and let stand 5 minutes to dissolve. Add the sugar, salt, and half the flour; beat well for 2 minutes. Beat in the egg and shortening. Add the remaining flour, and beat until smooth. Cover with a damp cloth, and let rise in refrigerator. Punch down and replace damp cloth.

About 2 hours before serving, grease a baking sheet. Cut off as much dough as you need, and shape into small rolls. Place the rolls on the baking sheet, cover with waxed paper and a kitchen towel, and let rise until doubled in size—about 1½ hours.

Preheat oven to 400°. Bake the rolls for 12 to 15 minutes, or until golden. Serve warm. Makes 36 to 40 rolls.

MUFFINS FROM BISCUIT MIX

These plain muffins become party fare when pieces of pear or pineapple are added to the dough before baking.

3 tablespoons sugar
2½ cups Homemade Biscuit Mix (page 248)
1 egg
¾ cup milk

Preheat oven to 425°. Grease 12 muffin cups. In a large bowl, stir together the sugar and biscuit mix. In a separate bowl, beat the egg and milk together well; add this to the dry ingredients, stirring quickly, until just moistened.

Spoon the mixture into greased muffin cups, filling each cup two-thirds full. Bake for 18 to 20 minutes, or until nicely browned. Makes 12.

WHOLE-WHEAT DATE MUFFINS

2 cups less 2 tablespoons whole-wheat flour
½ teaspoon salt
3 teaspoons baking powder
3 tablespoons pure vegetable oil
1 egg
1 cup milk
¼ cup honey
¼ cup pitted and chopped dates

Preheat oven to 400°. Grease 12 muffin cups. In a large bowl, combine the flour, salt, and baking powder. In a separate bowl or blender, blend together the oil, egg, milk, and honey; add this mixture to the dry ingredients, stirring only enough to moisten. Fold in the dates.

Spoon the mixture into greased muffin tins, filling each cup two-thirds full. Bake for 15 to 20 minutes, or until an uncolored toothpick inserted into the center comes out clean. Makes 9 to 12 muffins.

WHOLE-WHEAT MUFFINS

These are easily and quickly prepared and are good at any meal.

½ cup all-purpose flour	4 teaspoons baking powder
1 cup whole-wheat flour	1 egg, well beaten
¼ teaspoon salt	¾ cup milk

Preheat oven to 400°. Grease 10 muffin cups. In a large bowl, sift the flours together with the salt and baking powder. Beat in the egg and milk (the batter should be heavy).

Spoon the mixture into the muffin cups, filling each cup two-thirds full. Bake for 20 minutes. Makes 10 muffins.

CINNAMON RING

3 cups Homemade Biscuit Mix (page 248)	3 tablespoons ground cinnamon
1 cup sugar	½ cup sweet butter, melted

Heat oven to 450°. Generously grease a medium ring mold. On a floured board, roll out the biscuit mix to ½-inch thickness. Cut into biscuits.

In a small bowl, mix together the sugar and cinnamon. Dip each biscuit into the melted butter, then into the sugar mixture. Arrange the biscuits on edge all around the inside of the mold. Bake for 20 minutes, or until done. Let cool a little, then turn out onto a round plate or platter.

MARIANNE'S PUMPKIN SCONES

These are an American adaptation of the Australian scones served in Brisbane. Scones are like our own biscuits—whereas "biscuits" in Australia are what we call cookies.

½ cup canned pumpkin or prepared pumpkin
1 cup Homemade Biscuit Mix (page 248)

Preheat oven to 450°. In a medium bowl, add the pumpkin to the biscuit mixture, and mix together well. Turn out onto a lightly floured board, and knead a few times. With a floured rolling pin, roll out the dough ½ inch thick. With a 1½-inch cutter or the top of a small glass, cut the dough into biscuits. Place them 1 inch apart on an ungreased baking sheet. Bake for 8 to 10 minutes. Serve warm with Easy-To-Prepare Honey Butter (page 261) or ginger marmalade. Makes 10 to 12 scones.

BANANA-CARAMEL BUNS

From Minneapolis, the baking capital, comes another quickie using the Homemade Biscuit Mix on page 248.

½ cup brown sugar
6 tablespoons sweet butter
24 pecan halves
2 cups Homemade Biscuit Mix (page 248)
⅔ cup peeled and mashed bananas

Preheat oven to 450°. Grease 12 muffin cups. Place 1 teaspoon of the brown sugar, 1 teaspoon of the butter, and 2 pecan halves in the bottom of each of the muffin cups. Place the muffin tins in the oven just long enough to melt the butter and sugar. Set aside.

In a large bowl, stir together the biscuit mix and banana to make a soft dough. On a floured board, gently smooth the dough into a ball; knead 5 times. Roll the dough into a 9-by-15-inch rectangle.

In a saucepan, melt the remaining 2 tablespoons butter. Brush this over the dough, and sprinkle with the remaining brown sugar. Roll up the dough tightly, cut it into 12 pieces, and place each in a muffin cup. Bake for 10 minutes, or until an uncolored toothpick inserted in the center comes out clean. Remove from the oven, and immediately invert onto waxed paper. Serve warm. Makes 1 dozen.

BAKED PANCAKE PUFFS

6 eggs
1 cup milk
½ cup all-purpose flour
2 tablespoons sugar
1 teaspoon salt
2 tablespoons sweet butter
lemon juice, to taste
powdered sugar
honey

Preheat oven to 450°. In a large bowl, beat the eggs until light. Beat in the milk, flour, sugar, and salt until smooth.

Place 1 tablespoon of butter in each of two pie plates. Place the pie plates in the oven for 1 minute to heat the plates and melt the butter. Remove the plates, and swirl the melted butter around to coat the pan bottoms and sides.

Immediately pour the batter in equal amounts into the pie plates. Bake for 8 minutes. Reduce the heat to 375°, and bake for another 8 minutes, or until the pancakes are golden (the surface will be irregular, with high sides).

Remove the pancakes from the oven, and sprinkle each lightly with lemon juice, then dust with powdered sugar. Drizzle honey over each and serve immediately. These are also good with Norma's Pear Sauce (page 316). Serves 4.

✄———————————

WHOLE-WHEAT PANCAKES

¾–1 cup whole-wheat flour	1 cup milk
2 teaspoons baking powder	1 egg
½ teaspoon salt	1½ tablespoons pure
1 tablespoon honey	vegetable oil

In a medium bowl, combine ¾ cup of the flour, the baking powder, and the salt, and set aside. In a separate bowl, beat together the honey, milk, egg, and oil until smooth; stir this mixture into the dry ingredients only until moistened—do not overbeat. The batter should be the consistency of heavy cream; if too thin, add the remaining flour.

Slowly heat a griddle or heavy skillet to 400°. Test the temperature by dropping a little cold water on it; the water should roll off in drops. Grease the skillet, and pour in ⅛ cup batter for each pancake. Cook until bubbles form on the surface and the edges are dry. Turn the pancakes, and cook them for 2 minutes longer, or until they are browned. Serve hot with butter and honey or pure maple syrup. Makes 10 to 12 pancakes.

❦————————————————————————

VIRGINIA CORNMEAL PANCAKES

Served with additive-free ham or chicken, these would be equally good in place of corn bread or for breakfast.

1½ cups cornmeal	1 egg
½ cup all-purpose flour	1 cup milk
2 teaspoons baking powder	4 tablespoons sweet butter,
½ teaspoon salt	or bacon fat

In a medium bowl, sift together the cornmeal, flour, baking powder, and salt. In a separate bowl, beat the egg together with the milk, and stir this into the flour mixture. Let stand for 15 minutes. Stir the batter again, adding more milk if needed to give it a medium consistency—the batter should not be too thick.

Meanwhile, slowly heat a griddle or heavy skillet. Add the butter or fat and cook the pancakes as directed on page 255. Serve with pure maple syrup. Makes 12.

❦————————————————————————

NORWEGIAN PANCAKES

1 cup commercial sour cream	¾ cups sifted all-purpose flour
1 cup cottage cheese	1 tablespoon sugar
4 eggs	½ teaspoon salt

In a medium bowl, combine the sour cream and cottage cheese. Add the remaining ingredients, and beat until well mixed (the batter should be slightly lumpy).

Slowly heat a griddle or heavy skillet. Grease the skillet, and pour in 1 large tablespoon batter for each pancake. Cook the pancakes as directed on page 255. Serve plain or with butter and pure maple syrup. Makes 16 pancakes.

For Norwegian Pineapple Pancakes: To the batter, add 1 cup canned and well-drained crushed pineapple.

✿────────────────────────────

JOANN'S FAVORITE PANCAKES

An original recipe from Colorado, these pancakes are light, delicious, and simple to mix either in a small bowl or in a blender.

1 cup whole-wheat flour
1 cup milk
2 eggs
¼ cup cottage cheese
3 teaspoons baking powder

2 tablespoons pure vegetable oil
1 tablespoon sugar
½ teaspoon salt

Grease a skillet, and slowly heat it. In a mixing bowl or blender, mix all the ingredients together until blended (the batter should be slightly lumpy). Pour a few tablespoons of batter for each pancake onto the hot skillet. Cook until the edges of the pancakes begin to curl and dry. Turn the pancakes, and brown them on the other side. Serve warm, with or without syrup. Makes 12 pancakes.

BLINTZES

This is a recipe I've used for many years. Filled blintzes may be frozen and heated when needed.

PANCAKE BATTER:

2 eggs
1 cup water
½ teaspoon salt
⅔ cup all-purpose flour

FILLING:

1 pound dry cottage cheese
1 egg
1 teaspoon salt
1 tablespoon sweet butter, melted
½ teaspoon sugar

In a medium bowl, beat together the batter ingredients until well mixed and smooth. In a small skillet or crepe pan over low heat, melt about ½ teaspoon butter to lightly coat the pan. Pour in 1 tablespoon of the batter, and swirl the pan quickly to spread the batter. Cook the pancake on one side only until lightly browned. Remove it from the pan, melt another ½ teaspoon butter, and repeat the process until all batter is used. As each pancake is done, stack it between sheets of waxed paper.

To prepare the filling: In a medium bowl, mix together all the filling ingredients (the filling should be lumpy). In the center of the browned side of each pancake, place 1 tablespoon of the filling. Fold the sides over the mixture, and then fold the top and bottom up.

To bake, preheat oven to 350°. Grease a baking dish, and put in the filled blintzes side by side. Bake for 15 to 20 minutes, or until lightly browned.

To fry, heat a skillet, grease it with butter, and put in the filled blintzes side by side. Fry them on each side until lightly browned.

Serve hot, with sour cream. Makes 20 small blintzes.

EASY NO-HOLE DROP DOUGHNUTS

Another Baytown, Texas, recipe, these doughnuts take only about twenty minutes to make. Both children and adults will enjoy them.

2 cups pure vegetable oil for deep frying
2 eggs
½ cup sugar
2 tablespoons sweet butter, softened
2 cups all-purpose flour
2 teaspoons baking powder
½ teaspoon salt
½ cup milk

Preheat the oil in a deep-fat fryer to 375°. In a medium bowl, beat the eggs, then beat in the sugar and butter. In a separate bowl, sift together the flour, baking powder, and salt.

Stir the flour mixture into the egg and sugar mixture alternately with the milk. Using two spoons dipped in oil so that the dough will slide off easily, drop the batter by teaspoonfuls into the hot oil. Turn the doughnuts to brown them evenly, and remove with a slotted spoon. Drain on paper towels. Makes about 48.

ℋ ────────

WAFFLES

Here is another recipe that calls for Homemade Biscuit Mix.

2 cups Homemade Biscuit
  Mix (page 248)
1½ cups milk or buttermilk
1 egg, well beaten

2 tablespoons sweet butter,
  melted
1 teaspoon sugar
pinch of salt

Preheat a waffle iron. In a large bowl, beat together all the ingredients until well blended.

Pour about ⅓ cup batter onto the waffle iron (the batter should spread to within 1 inch of the edges). Lower the cover, and cook according to the manufacturer's directions, or until the iron stops steaming. Loosen the waffle edges with a fork and carefully remove. Serve with butter and honey or pure maple syrup. Serves 6.

ℋ ──────────────────

BUTTERSCOTCH OATMEAL

2 eggs, beaten
3½ cups milk
½ cup honey

2 cups quick-cooking rolled
  oats
4 tablespoons sweet butter

In a saucepan, combine the eggs, milk, and honey. Cook, stirring, over medium heat for about 5 minutes. Stir in the oats, and cook for 5 minutes longer, or until done. Add the butter, cover, and remove from the heat. Let stand for a few minutes. Stir and serve. Serves 4 to 6.

BAKED FRENCH TOAST

6 tablespoons sweet butter 1 cup milk
4 eggs 8 slices pure white bread
½ teaspoon salt

Preheat oven to 475°. Grease a baking sheet with 2 tablespoons of the butter.

In a flat, shallow dish, beat together the eggs, salt, and milk. Dip each bread slice into the egg mixture, turning once and making sure the bread is thoroughly saturated. Arrange the bread slices in a single layer on the baking sheet.

In a small saucepan, slowly melt the remaining butter, and just before baking drizzle it over the slices. Bake for 5 minutes on one side, turn, and bake for another 5 minutes, or until golden brown. Serve at once with pure maple syrup, honey, any permitted jam, or cinnamon sugar. Serves 4.

EASY-TO-PREPARE HONEY BUTTER

Your children, hyperactive or not, will find this delicious served on toast.

1 egg yolk 1 cup honey
½ cup sweet butter

Place all the ingredients in a blender, and blend on medium speed for 35 seconds. Store, covered, in the refrigerator.

❦————————————————————

CINNAMON-BUTTER BALLS

These are perfect with fancy breads such as the rich Date-Nut Bread on page 239.

¼ pound sweet butter,
softened

2 teaspoons ground
cinnamon

In a small bowl, cream the butter together with the cinnamon. Form the mixture into small balls. Place on an ungreased baking sheet, cover, and freeze until firm or until needed. Serve somewhat softened. Makes 8 balls.

❦————————————————————

CLEO JEPPSON'S BREAD CRUMBS

For the many recipes that call for bread crumbs, this recipe should prove invaluable. These bread crumbs can be stored for weeks in a paper bag if kept perfectly dry. Do not use an airtight container because even a small amount of moisture can get into these containers and cause mildew.

For this recipe, use soft, day-old pure bread slices or leftover crusts. Two slices or 1 slice plus the crusts from 2 pieces of bread makes ½ cup of bread crumbs.

Preheat oven to 300°. Tear the slices, one at a time, into small pieces, and place them in a blender container. Blend at medium speed or on "grate" until the bread is well crumbed. Repeat until all the slices are crumbed.

Place the crumbs on an ungreased shallow baking pan, and bake for 30 minutes, watching carefully that they don't burn. Remove from the oven; let stand until very dry.

Store in a paper bag in a dry place at room temperature.

BEVERAGES

Serve these in sherbet cups or wineglasses. You can also make popsicles from any of the icy recipes. Simply pour the mixture into ice cube trays or popsicle containers, add a wooden popsicle stick, if available, to each cube, and freeze. Bear in mind that if you plan to freeze these desserts, you should use slightly less sugar. Always serve icies as soon as they are ready.

PINK ICY

1 can Seven-Up
1 tablespoon sugar

1 teaspoon beet juice
1 teaspoon lemon juice

Fill half the blender with ice. Add all the ingredients, and blend on low speed, then beat on high until thick and frothy. Serves 2 generously. Serve at once.

LEMON ICY

*½ 6-ounce can frozen
   lemonade concentrate
   (check the label)*

¼ cup sugar
1 cup milk

Fill half the blender with ice. Add all the ingredients, and blend on low speed, then beat on high until thick and frothy. Serves 2.

CAROB ICY

*2 tablespoons carob
   powder (check the label)*

1 tablespoon sugar
1 cup milk

Fill half the blender with ice. Add all the ingredients, and blend on low speed, then beat on high until thick. Serves 1.

PINEAPPLE ICY

½ cup unsweetened crushed pineapple with juice
¼ cup sugar
1 cup milk

Fill half the blender with ice. Add all the ingredients, and blend on low speed, then beat on high until thick. Serves 2.

FROSTED COCKTAIL

½ cup sugar
⅔ cup water
⅔ cup lemon juice
⅔ cup pineapple juice
2 tablespoons lime juice
2 egg whites
4 cups finely crushed ice

In a medium saucepan, combine the sugar and the water, and cook for 5 minutes. Chill for at least 1 hour. Add all the remaining ingredients. Pour half the mixture into a blender and blend until light and frothy, about 7 or 8 seconds. Repeat with the remainder of the mixture. Serve at once in chilled cocktail glasses. Serves 8 to 10.

CANTALOUPE COOLER

This recipe can also be frozen into popsicles in popsicle containers or ice cube trays.

½ cup unsweetened
   pineapple juice

2 cups cubed ripe cantaloupe
2 ice cubes

Pour the pineapple juice into a blender. With the blender set at medium speed, drop the cantaloupe cubes into the container, a few pieces at a time, blending well. Add ice cubes and blend. Makes 2½ cups.

✣ SPEEDY BREAKFAST NOG

1½ cups pineapple juice
1 egg

1 tablespoon honey

In a blender combine all the ingredients. Blend for 1 minute to mix well. Makes 2 servings.

✣ SUNSHINE CARROT COCKTAIL

2 cups pineapple juice
3 medium carrots, peeled
   and cut into 2-inch pieces

¾ banana, peeled and
   cut up
4–6 ice cubes

Put all the ingredients except for the ice cubes into a blender. Blend on high speed until the carrots are liquefied. Add the ice cubes, one at a time, blending well. Serve immediately. Makes 4 cups.

✿

DONNA'S BANANA NOG

*1 ripe banana, peeled and
    cut up*
1 cup milk

1 teaspoon honey
1 cup ice cubes
¼ teaspoon nutmeg

Put all the ingredients except for the nutmeg into a blender, and blend at high speed for 30 seconds. Pour into tall glasses, dust with the nutmeg, and serve at once. Serves 2.

✿

SAN DIEGO EGG NOG

2 cups milk
1 egg

1 teaspoon honey
½ teaspoon pure vanilla

Put all the ingredients into a blender, and blend on medium speed until frothy. Serves 2.

CAKES

NORMA'S CAKE MIX

This homemade cake mix is a real time saver for the busy homemaker. It should be kept on hand and used as needed.

6 cups sifted all-purpose flour	2 tablespoons baking powder
3 cups sugar	1 teaspoon salt
½ cup nonfat dry milk powder	1½ cups solid Crisco shortening

Place the first five ingredients in a large bowl. Cut or mix in the shortening until the mix is fine and crumbly, the consistency of a packaged mix. Store, tightly covered, at room temperature or in the refrigerator. Will make 3 layer cakes.

FOR A LARGE CAKE

3 cups Norma's Cake Mix	½ cup water
2 eggs	

Preheat oven to 350°. Grease two round cake pans or one large square pan.

In a large bowl, combine the cake mix with the eggs and the water, and stir until blended. Pour the batter into the cake pans, and bake for 25 to 30 minutes, or until an uncolored toothpick inserted in the center comes out clean.

FOR A SMALL CAKE

1½ cups Norma's Cake Mix	⅓ cup water
1 egg	

Preheat oven to 350°. Grease a small cake pan.

In a medium bowl, combine the cake mix with the egg

and the water, and stir until blended. Pour the batter into the cake pan, and bake for 20 to 25 minutes, or until an uncolored toothpick inserted in the center comes out clean.

�֍————————————————————————

FANNY'S SPICY CARROT CAKE

This keeps well if wrapped in foil and frozen, and is particularly good for holiday dinners. Glaze just before serving.

1½ cups pure vegetable oil
2½ cups sugar
4 eggs, separated
5 tablespoons very hot water
2½ cups all-purpose flour
1½ teaspoons baking powder

½ teaspoon baking soda
¼ teaspoon salt
1 teaspoon ground cinnamon
1½ cups peeled, grated, and firmly packed carrots
1 cup chopped walnuts

LEMON GLAZE:

¾ cup powdered sugar   2 tablespoons lemon juice

————————————————————————

Preheat oven to 350°. Grease and flour a large angel-food cake pan.

In a large bowl of an electric mixer, beat the oil and sugar at medium speed until well mixed. Beat in the egg yolks, one at a time, beating well after each addition. Beat in the water.

In a separate bowl, sift together the flour, baking powder, baking soda, salt, and cinnamon. Add this to the egg mixture, and beat well. Stir in the grated carrots and chopped nuts; mix well. Beat the egg whites to a soft peak, and fold them into the batter.

Pour the batter into the prepared pan, and bake for 70 minutes. Let cool for 15 minutes, then turn out onto a plate to cool for 5 minutes more before glazing.

Meanwhile, to prepare the lemon glaze: In a small bowl, beat together the powdered sugar and lemon juice. Drizzle over the top of the cake.

❀ QUICK-MIX BANANA CAKE

Not only easy and quick, this cake made with honey and whole-wheat flour is also nutritious.

3 eggs
⅔ cup honey
3 bananas, peeled and
  cut up
1 teaspoon pure vanilla

½ cup pure vegetable oil
½ cup chopped walnuts
2 heaping cups whole-wheat
  flour
1 tablespoon baking powder

ICING

1 3-ounce package cream
  cheese, softened

2 tablespoons milk

Preheat oven to 325°. Grease a 9-by-13-inch baking pan. In a blender container, combine the eggs, honey, bananas, vanilla, and oil; blend until smooth. Add the walnuts; turn the blender on and off quickly to just mix.

In a large bowl, stir together the whole-wheat flour and baking powder. Pour the blender mixture over the flour, and mix together well. Pour the batter into the baking pan, and bake for about 30 minutes, or until an uncolored toothpick inserted in the center comes out clean. Let cool on a wire rack.

Meanwhile, to prepare the icing: In a small bowl, beat together the icing ingredients. Frost the cake when cooled.

✂——————————————————————————

PARTY NEW ORLEANS COFFEE CAKE

TOPPING:

½ cup brown sugar
1 tablespoon ground
cinnamon

3 tablespoons sweet butter,
melted
¾ cup chopped walnuts

CAKE:

½ cup sweet butter,
softened
1¼ cups sugar
2 eggs
2 teaspoons grated lemon
rind

2¼ cups all-purpose flour
½ teaspoon baking soda
½ teaspoon salt
1 cup milk

———————————————————————————

Preheat oven to 350°. Grease a 13-by-9-by-2-inch baking pan. In a small bowl, combine the brown sugar, cinnamon, butter, and walnuts. Mix together well, and set aside.

In a large bowl, cream together the butter, sugar, and eggs; stir in the lemon rind. In a separate bowl, sift together the flour, baking soda, and salt. Beginning and ending with the flour, beat in the flour, one-quarter at a time, alternately with the milk, into the butter-sugar mixture.

Pour half the batter into the baking pan, and spread evenly with a spatula. Sprinkle with half the topping. Add the remaining batter, spread carefully, and sprinkle with the remaining topping. Bake for 30 to 40 minutes, or until the cake springs back when pressed in the center and an un-colored toothpick inserted in the center comes out clean. Serves 12.

✂————————————————————

CHOCOLATE SNACK CAKE

1⅔ cups all-purpose flour
1 cup firmly packed brown
  sugar
¼ cup cocoa
  (check the label)
1 teaspoon baking soda
½ teaspoon salt

1 cup water
⅓ cup pure vegetable oil
1 teaspoon white distilled
  vinegar
½ teaspoon pure vanilla
powdered sugar (optional)

Preheat oven to 350°. In a medium bowl, mix the flour, brown sugar, cocoa, baking soda, and salt with a fork. Stir in the water, the oil, the vinegar, and the vanilla; mix together thoroughly. Pour into an ungreased 8-by-8-by-2-inch baking pan. Bake for 35 to 40 minutes, or until an uncolored toothpick inserted in the center comes out clean. Dust with powdered sugar if desired.

✂————————————————————

FIG-CARROT CAKE, HOUSTON

This is a moist cake that needs no icing and uses less sugar than some of the vegetable breads.

1½ cups all-purpose flour
1 cup sugar
1 teaspoon baking powder
1 teaspoon baking soda
¼ teaspoon ground
  cinnamon
¼ teaspoon salt
⅔ cup pure vegetable oil

2 eggs
1 teaspoon pure vanilla
1 cup peeled and
  finely shredded carrots
½ cup unsweetened
  shredded coconut
¾ cup figs, cut into small
  pieces

Preheat oven to 350°. Grease and flour a bundt pan.

In a large bowl, combine the first nine ingredients; beat for 2 minutes, or until well blended. Add the carrots, coconut, and figs, and mix together well.

Pour the batter into the bundt pan, and bake for 45 minutes, or until an uncolored toothpick inserted in the center comes out clean. Cool in the pan for 10 to 15 minutes, then turn out onto a wire rack to complete the cooling.

GRAPEFRUIT CAKE

May McIntyre, of Vernon, British Columbia, shares this unusual cake recipe, which is perfect for the diet. This recipe makes a very large cake and can be cut in half.

3¾ cups sifted all-purpose flour
1 tablespoon baking powder
½ teaspoon baking soda
½ teaspoon salt
2 cups sugar
1 cup solid Crisco shortening, softened
4 eggs
1 egg yolk
¾ cup unsweetened grapefruit juice

Preheat oven to 350°. Grease and flour three 9-inch layer pans or one angel-food cake pan. In a large bowl, sift together the dry ingredients; set aside.

In a separate bowl, cream the sugar together with the shortening. Beat in the eggs, one at a time, and the egg yolk. Into the shortening mixture, beat the dry ingredients alternately with the grapefruit juice. Pour the batter into the pans, and bake for 30 to 35 minutes, or until an uncolored toothpick inserted in the center comes out clean. Cool on a wire rack.

✂ ————————————
RHUBARB CAKE

This makes a delicious, moist cake. If frozen rhubarb is used, defrost it, and cut it into small pieces before baking.

1½ cups brown sugar
½ cup solid Crisco
  shortening
1 egg
1 teaspoon pure vanilla
1 teaspoon salt

2 cups all-purpose flour
1 teaspoon baking soda
1 cup buttermilk or
  sour whole milk
2 cups chopped rhubarb

TOPPING

1 tablespoon ground
  cinnamon

¼ cup sugar

Preheat oven to 350°. Grease a 9-by-13-inch baking pan. In a large bowl, cream the sugar and shortening together. Beat in the egg and vanilla. In a separate bowl, sift together the salt, flour, and baking soda; add this dry mixture to the sugar and shortening mixture. Beat in the buttermilk and rhubarb. Pour the batter into the pan.

In a small bowl, mix together the topping ingredients. Sprinkle the mixture over the batter. Bake for 45 minutes. Serve either hot or cold, with pure whipped cream.

✂ ————————————
FREDA'S SPONGE CAKE

4 eggs, separated
1 cup sifted sugar
3 teaspoons baking powder

1½ cups all-purpose flour
1 teaspoon pure vanilla
¾ cup water

Preheat oven to 325°. In a large bowl, beat the egg yolks until they are light in color but thick. Gradually add the sugar and continue beating. In a separate bowl, sift together the baking powder with ½ cup of the flour.

To the egg and sugar mixture, alternately beat in the vanilla, the water, and the remaining 1 cup flour. Add the baking powder and flour mixture.

Beat the egg whites until stiff. Carefully fold them into the batter. Gently turn into an ungreased angel-food cake pan, and bake for 45 minutes, or until an uncolored toothpick inserted in the center comes out clean. When done, invert the pan until cool.

✠───────────────

MY FRIEND IRMA'S SCHNECKEN

This dough must be started the day before baking. Because it is a very light, moist dough, it is not easy to handle, but it makes an excellent pastry that freezes well and is not too sweet. This is a recipe for an experienced baker.

1 cube fresh yeast
1 cup plus 1 teaspoon sugar
½ cup lukewarm water
12 tablespoons sweet butter
3½ cups all-purpose flour
½ teaspoon salt

2 eggs, slightly beaten
1 cup milk, scalded
2 teaspoons ground
  cinnamon
36 whole walnuts

GLAZE

4 tablespoons sweet butter,
  melted

½ cup dark brown sugar
1 teaspoon water

In a small bowl, crumble the yeast cube, and sprinkle it with 1 teaspoon of the sugar; pour in the warm water and let stand for 5 minutes to dissolve (don't stir).

Meanwhile, in a large bowl, cream 8 tablespoons of the butter with ½ cup of the sugar. Add the flour and salt, and mix with a fork. Make a well in the center of this mixture; add the eggs, one at a time, beating them in lightly with a fork. Beat in the yeast mixture. Add the milk, and knead until the dough lifts from the bowl. Knead in the bowl by hand, or with an electric mixer or a wooden spoon. By hand this should take 10 minutes, with a mixer less time. Butter one side of a large piece of waxed paper, and place it, butter side down, over the bowl. Cover with a towel, and let stand overnight in a cool place.

In the morning, work the dough again. Let stand for 1½ hours. On a well-floured board or counter top, roll out the dough. With floured hands, pat the dough into a large rectangle about ½ inch thick.

In a small saucepan, melt the remaining 4 tablespoons butter; add the remaining ½ cup sugar and the cinnamon, and brush this mixture evenly over the dough.

Grease 3 dozen muffin cups, and place a walnut in the bottom of each cup. In a small bowl, mix the glaze ingredients together with 1 teaspoon of water. Spoon 1 teaspoon of glaze into each muffin cup.

Roll up the dough tightly; slice the schnecken into ½-inch-wide pieces. Place each piece in a muffin cup, and let rise for 1 hour.

Preheat oven to 350°. Bake the schnecken for 20 to 25 minutes. Cool for 1 minute, then remove from the tins. Reheat just before serving. Makes 36.

❦ ────────────────────────────────

HENNIE'S DATE AND NUT SLICES

When my mother entertained the ladies at luncheon, this was the dessert she served. It is as rich as pecan pie but easier to prepare and contains less sugar.

2 eggs
½ cup sugar
2 tablespoons half-and-half
2 tablespoons all-purpose
  flour
1 teaspoon baking powder

½ teaspoon pure vanilla
1 cup chopped walnuts
1 cup pitted dates,
  cut into small pieces
whipped cream

────────────────────────────────

Preheat oven to 325°. Grease a square baking pan. In a large bowl, beat the eggs until light and lemon colored. Add the sugar and the half-and-half, and continue beating until well blended.

In a cup, mix the flour with the baking powder; stir this into the egg mixture. Stir in the vanilla, walnuts, and dates. Pour the mixture into the baking pan, and bake for 30 minutes. Let cool slightly, then cut into 2-by-4-inch bars. Serve with whipped cream on top. Serves 6.

COOKIES

½ cup sweet butter,
  softened
1 cup pure peanut butter
½ cup sugar
½ cup firmly packed brown
  sugar

½ teaspoon pure vanilla
1 egg
1½ cups all-purpose flour
¾ teaspoon baking soda
½ teaspoon baking powder
¼ teaspoon salt

In a large bowl, cream together the butter and peanut butter. Gradually add the sugars, and cream all together until light and fluffy. Add the vanilla and egg, and beat well.

In a separate bowl, sift together the flour, baking soda, baking powder, and salt. Stir these dry ingredients into the peanut butter mixture, and mix together thoroughly. Cover the dough with waxed paper, and chill in the refrigerator for 30 minutes.

Preheat oven to 375°. Grease a large baking sheet. Shape the dough into small balls, and place them about 2 inches apart on the baking sheet. Flatten them with a fork in a crisscross pattern. Bake for 10 to 12 minutes. Makes about 5 dozen.

ℋ————

PUFFED WHEAT COOKIES

Brian from Minnesota is only nine years old, but with supervision he made this for his Cub Scout peers.

¼ cup pure vegetable oil
½ cup honey
¼ cup pure peanut butter
1 tablespoon unsulphured
  molasses
1 egg
1 tablespoon milk
½ teaspoon salt
1 teaspoon baking powder

½ teaspoon baking soda
1½ cups all-purpose flour
1 cup puffed wheat cereal
  (check the label)
¼ cup chopped nuts
  (any kind except almonds)
1 bar Baker's German's Sweet
  Chocolate (optional)

Preheat oven to 350°. Grease a baking sheet. In a large bowl, mix all the ingredients together well, except for the chocolate. Drop the mixture by teaspoonfuls onto the baking sheet. Bake for 10 to 12 minutes, or until the edges are browned. Let cool.

Meanwhile, if a chocolate frosting is desired, in the top of a double boiler over boiling water, melt the chocolate. Frost the cookies. Makes about 3 dozen.

ℋ————

COOKIES FROM TUCSON

1 cup sweet butter, softened
½ cup sugar
1 egg, separated
1 teaspoon pure vanilla
2 cups sifted all-purpose
  flour

¼ cup brown sugar
2 tablespoons finely
  chopped nuts
  (any kind except almonds)
dash of ground cinnamon

Preheat oven to 350°. In a large bowl, cream together the butter and sugar. Add the egg yolk, vanilla, and flour, and mix until well blended. Shape the dough into small balls about the size of marbles. Place on an ungreased baking sheet.

In a small bowl, beat the egg white slightly; dip a fork in the white, and press the cookies down with the tines.

In another small bowl, combine the brown sugar, nuts, and cinnamon. Sprinkle this mixture over the cookies. Bake for 10 minutes, or until the cookies are very lightly browned. Makes about 13 dozen small cookies.

CY'S SAN FRANCISCO COOKIES

1 cup brown sugar	*1 teaspoon salt*
1 cup all-purpose flour	*⅛ teaspoon baking soda*
1 egg	*1 cup chopped walnuts*

Preheat oven to 350°. Grease an 8-inch-square baking pan. In a large bowl, mix all the ingredients together. Pour the mixture into the pan, and bake for 20 minutes, or until an uncolored toothpick inserted in the center comes out clean. Cool in the pan. Cut into 2-inch squares. Makes 16.

EASY-MIX CHOCOLATE DROP COOKIES

1 cup brown sugar
½ cup butter
1 egg
6 tablespoons cocoa
  (check the label)
½ cup milk
1½ teaspoons pure vanilla

2 cups sifted all-purpose
  flour
½ teaspoon baking soda
dash of salt
⅔ cup chopped nuts
  (any kind except almonds)

Preheat oven to 350°. In a large bowl or electric mixer combine all the ingredients except for the nuts. Beat at medium speed for 4 to 5 minutes. Stir in the nuts. Drop by teaspoonfuls onto ungreased baking sheets. Bake for 8 to 10 minutes. Makes 3 to 4 dozen.

SUPER FUDGE

1 cup honey
1 cup pure peanut butter
1 cup carob powder
  (check the label)
1 cup sesame seeds

1 cup sunflower seeds
½ cup shredded
  unsweetened coconut
½ cup chopped dates

Grease two 8-by-8-by-2-inch baking pans. In a saucepan over low heat, heat the honey together with the peanut butter. Quickly stir in the carob powder and the seeds, coconut, and dates. Pour the mixture into the pans, and refrigerate until hardened—at least 1 hour. Cut into 1-inch squares. Store, covered with waxed paper, in the refrigerator. Makes 84 pieces.

�֍──────────────────

CHOCOLATE-COCONUT CHEWS

The fastest bake in the West.

1 egg
2 egg whites
1 3½-ounce can shredded unsweetened coconut
¾ cup sugar

½ cup chopped walnuts or pecans
1 teaspoon pure vanilla
2 squares Baker's Unsweetened Chocolate

Preheat oven to 350°. Grease a baking sheet well. In a medium bowl, mix together all the ingredients except for the chocolate, and set aside. In the top of a large double boiler, over hot but not boiling water, melt the chocolate; immediately stir in the coconut mixture. Drop by rounded teaspoonfuls, about 1 inch apart, onto the baking sheet. Bake for 12 minutes, or until the chews are set. Makes about 2 dozen cookies.

�֍──────────────────

SUSIE'S CARROT COOKIES

This Tulsa, Oklahoma, recipe calls for less sugar so that it is more acceptable as a snack or for dessert.

¾ cup sugar
¾ cup solid Crisco shortening
1 egg

1 cup peeled, cooked, and mashed carrots
2 cups sifted all-purpose flour
2 teaspoons baking powder

Preheat oven to 350°. Grease a baking sheet. In a medium bowl, cream together the sugar and shortening. Beat in the egg and carrots. Add the flour and baking powder, and stir until well mixed.

Drop by teaspoonfuls onto the baking sheet. Bake for 18 to 20 minutes. Makes about 5½ dozen.

PUMPKIN COOKIES

Jean Berk's class at the Ocean City, New Jersey, Intermediate School made these cookies for their Halloween treat.

2 cups all-purpose flour
1 teaspoon baking powder
1 teaspoon baking soda
1 teaspoon ground cinnamon
½ teaspoon salt
1 cup sweet butter, softened
1 cup sugar
1 egg, beaten
1 cup canned or prepared pumpkin (see Note)
1 cup chopped nuts (any kind except almonds)
1 teaspoon pure vanilla

Preheat oven to 350°. Grease two baking sheets. In a large bowl, sift the flour with the baking powder, baking soda, cinnamon, and salt. Set aside.

In a separate bowl, cream the butter at medium speed until light. Gradually beat in the sugar, then the egg and pumpkin, beating until smooth. Add the flour mixture, and beat, at low speed or by hand, until well mixed. Stir in the nuts and vanilla. Drop by rounded teaspoonfuls, about 2 inches apart, onto the baking sheets. Bake for 12 to 15 minutes, or until lightly browned. Makes about 8 dozen.

Note: To prepare pumpkin meat, scoop out the insides of a pumpkin, reserving the seeds to make Roasted Pumpkin Seeds, below. Preheat oven to 350°. Cut the pumpkin meat into large pieces, and wrap them in aluminum foil. Place the pieces on a baking sheet, and bake for 1 hour, or until soft. Press through a sieve. Can be frozen until needed.

⌘————————————————

ROASTED PUMPKIN SEEDS

2 cups raw pumpkin seeds	*1½ tablespoons pure*
1 teaspoon salt	*vegetable oil*

Preheat oven to 250°. Wipe the seeds dry on paper towels, removing any membranes. In a medium bowl, mix the seeds well with the salt and oil. Spread them on an ungreased baking sheet, and roast, stirring occasionally, until browned —about 30 minutes. Makes 2 cups.

⌘————————————————

ALLEN'S LEMONADE COOKIES

These cookies have a delightful lemon flavor.

1 cup sweet butter, softened	*3 cups all-purpose flour*
1 cup sugar	*1 6-ounce can frozen*
2 eggs	*lemonade concentrate,*
1 teaspoon baking soda	*thawed (check the label)*

Preheat oven to 400°. In a large bowl, cream the butter together with the sugar. Add the eggs, and beat well. In a separate bowl, sift together the baking soda and flour; stir this into the egg mixture alternately with ½ cup of the lemonade concentrate. Drop by teaspoonfuls, 2 inches apart, on ungreased baking sheets. Bake for 8 minutes, or until the cookie edges are golden. After removing from the oven, brush the cookies lightly with the remaining 2 ounces lemonade concentrate. Cool. Makes about 6 dozen.

✿————————————

JAM OR JELLY SLICES

An Australian parent provided this recipe for easy cookies. Use any permitted jam, such as fig or pineapple, or any jelly, such as guava.

½ cup sweet butter	*1 cup all-purpose flour*
¾ cup brown sugar	*1 cup uncooked rolled oats*
¼ cup permitted jam or jelly	*2–4 tablespoons water*

Preheat oven to 325°. Grease a 9-by-4-inch loaf pan. In a saucepan over low heat, melt the butter. Add the sugar and the jam or jelly, and cook, stirring, until the mixture is smooth. Remove from the heat.

Stir in the flour, oats, and 2 tablespoons of water to make a moist, doughy batter, adding a tablespoon or two more water if necessary. Pour the batter into the loaf pan, and bake for 30 to 35 minutes. Cut into ½-inch slices, then cut the slices in half. Cool in the pan. Makes 2 dozen.

FRANCES'S CHEESECAKE COOKIES

These are excellent cookies that do not contain very much sugar.

⅓ cup sweet butter, softened
⅓ cup firmly packed brown sugar
1 cup all-purpose flour
¼ teaspoon baking powder
¼ teaspoon salt
½ cup chopped walnuts or pecans
½ pound cream cheese, softened
¼ cup granulated sugar
1 egg
2 tablespoons milk
1 tablespoon lemon juice
½ teaspoon pure vanilla

Preheat oven to 350°. Grease an 8-inch-square baking pan. In a large bowl, cream together the butter and brown sugar. In a separate bowl, sift together the flour, baking powder, and salt; stir this into the butter mixture. Add the nuts, and blend with your fingers until crumbly. Lightly press half the mixture into the pan; set the remainder aside. Bake for 15 minutes, or until golden brown at the edges. Let cool.

In a medium bowl, blend the cream cheese and granulated sugar. Add the egg, milk, lemon juice, and vanilla, and beat until smooth. Spread the mixture over the baked crust. Sprinkle with the reserved crumbs. Bake for 25 to 30 minutes, or until an uncolored toothpick inserted in the center comes out clean. Let cool to room temperature. Cover, and refrigerate until ready to serve. To serve, cut into bite-sized squares. Makes about 50 small cookies.

❤───────────

SCOTCH SHORTBREAD

1 cup sweet butter, softened   2 cups sifted all-purpose
¾ cup sifted powdered   flour
   sugar

─────────────────────────────────

Preheat oven to 300°. In a large bowl, cream the butter. Stir in the sugar and flour. Divide the mixture into two dough balls. On a floured board, pat each ball into a circle ¼ inch thick. Pinch the edges with your fingers to flute like a pie-crust. Prick the dough circles with the tines of a fork, and place them on an ungreased baking sheet. Bake for 45 minutes, or until lightly browned. Let cool, then cut into pie-shaped wedges. Makes about 20.

❤───────────

MADELEINES

3 large eggs   2 teaspoons grated lemon
¾ cup sugar   rind
1 teaspoon pure vanilla   ¾ cup sweet butter, melted
1 cup sifted cake flour

─────────────────────────────────

Preheat oven to 400°. Butter muffin cups thoroughly. In a large bowl of an electric mixer, work the eggs, sugar, and vanilla together with a wooden spoon. Place the bowl over barely simmering water, stirring constantly, until the mixture is lukewarm, not hot. Remove from heat.

    With the electric mixer at high speed, beat until light, fluffy, and creamy and the mixture has tripled in volume—at least 5 to 10 minutes. Gently fold in the flour, lemon rind and melted butter—do not beat. Continue gently folding until no dry flour or butter remains.

Fill the muffin cups with the mixture. Bake for 8 to 10 minutes, or until an uncolored toothpick inserted in the center comes out clean. Remove the cakes to cool on a rack. Store in a tightly covered container. Makes 36 madeleines.

❃————————————————

OATMEAL COOKIES

These oatmeal cookies are delicious with the addition of grated carrots; with any seeds, especially poppy seeds; or with cut-up, dried fruits such as figs or dates.

¾ cup sweet butter, softened	1 cup whole-wheat flour
⅔ cup honey	2 teaspoons baking powder
2 eggs	3 cups uncooked rolled oats
2 teaspoons pure vanilla	½ cup chopped walnuts
½ teaspoon salt	½ cup shredded unsweetened coconut

Preheat oven to 325°. Grease a baking sheet. In a large bowl, cream together the butter, honey, eggs, and vanilla. In a separate bowl, stir together the salt, flour, baking powder, and oats. Combine the dry ingredients with the creamed mixture. Add the nuts and coconut, and mix together thoroughly. Drop by rounded teaspoonfuls onto the baking sheet. Bake for 10 minutes. Makes about 3 or 4 dozen cookies.

❀————————————————————

GRANOLA COOKIES

1 cup pure vegetable oil
1 cup honey
2 eggs
1 cup chopped pecans or
  unsalted sunflower seeds
1 teaspoon pure vanilla

2 cups whole-wheat flour
½ teaspoon salt
2½ cups granola
  (check the label) or
  Betti's Granola (page 63)

Preheat oven to 300°. Grease a baking sheet. In a large bowl, mix the oil and honey. Add the eggs, pecans, and vanilla. Sift in the flour and salt, and then stir in the granola until well mixed. Drop by teaspoonfuls onto the baking sheet. Bake for 15 minutes for moister cookies, 20 minutes for crunchier cookies. Makes 3 to 4 dozen.

❀————————————————————

MINNESOTA GRANOLA BARS

A child can make this, it is so easy and such fun.

¼ cup honey
½ cup pure peanut butter
2 large eggs
¼ cup sweet butter
1 cup chopped nuts (any
  kind except almonds)

3 cups granola
  (check the label) or
  Betti's Granola (page 63)

Grease a 9-inch loaf pan. In a saucepan, mix together the honey and peanut butter. Beat in the eggs, one at a time. Cook, stirring constantly, over medium heat, until the mixture boils and leaves the sides of the pan. Remove from heat, and stir in the butter. Add the nuts and granola, and mix together well. Press the mixture into the pan, and chill. Cut into ½-inch bars. Makes 18.

PIES AND
OTHER DESSERTS